LOST RAIl
OF
DEVON

Stan Yorke

COUNTRYSIDE BOOKS
NEWBURY, BERKSHIRE

First published 2007
© Stan Yorke, 2007

COUNTRYSIDE BOOKS
3 Catherine Road
Newbury, Berkshire

To view our complete range of books,
please visit us at
www.countrysidebooks.co.uk

ISBN 978 1 85306 926 0

The cover picture shows West Country Class loco,
No 34001 'Exeter' travelling towards Ilfracombe in 1952
and is from an original painting by
Colin Doggett

Designed by Mon Mohan
Produced through MRM Associates Ltd., Reading
Typeset by CJWT Solutions, St Helens
Printed by Cambridge University Press

*All material for the manufacture of this book
was sourced from sustainable forests.*

CONTENTS

NOTES ON THE MAPS

All the maps use the same simple designation – a solid line for routes that have always carried a passenger service and a dotted line for those that are either goods only or closed. In order to conserve space the term 'Halt' has been omitted from station names.

ABBREVIATIONS

The following abbreviations are used in this book:

BR	British Rail (British Railways prior to 1965)
DMU	Diesel multiple unit
GWR	Great Western Railway
LSWR	London & South Western Railway
SR	Southern Railway

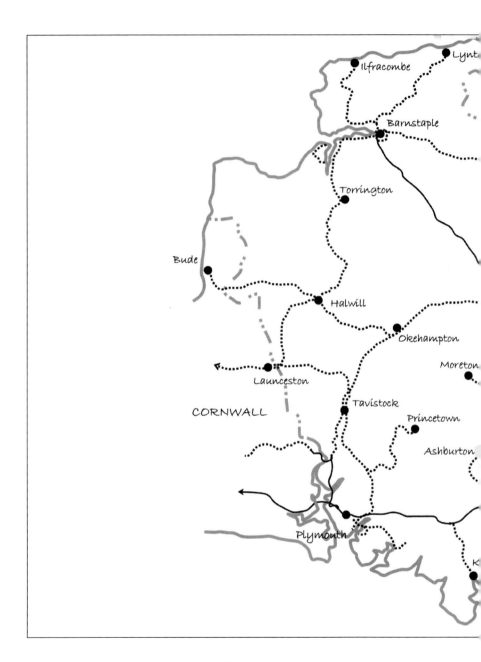

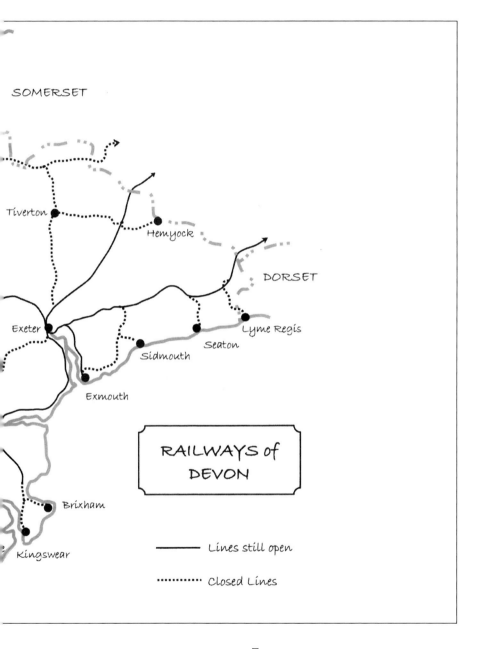

SOMERSET

Tiverton

Hemyock

DORSET

Exeter

Lyme Regis

Sidmouth

Seaton

Exmouth

RAILWAYS of
DEVON

Brixham

Kingswear

———— Lines still open

·············· Closed Lines

Introduction

To most of us the name Devon probably conjures up cream teas and holidays rather than hissing engines and rattling coaches. Indeed Devon had relatively little industry that we would naturally associate with railways other than possibly the docks in Plymouth.

This pastoral image is indeed reflected in the history of its railway lines. The main line from London reached Exeter in 1844 and Plymouth in 1848. Barnstaple was linked to Exeter in 1854, thus connecting the three major centres of population. But what drove the construction of the other 400-odd route miles of railways and what characterised these lines that caused them to almost entirely disappear before the end of the 20th century?

They were basically built to serve just two kinds of customers, the people in the rural villages and tourists, both of whom eventually succumbed to motor transport. In the Victorian era rail travel revolutionised journey times – a tiresome four-hour ride by horse-drawn coach became a relatively comfortable one-hour trip. So even if your station was a mile from the village or a mile from the seaside town and you had to complete your journey by cart or coach, the reduction in the journey time was still dramatic. However, in the new world of the car and lorry, combining modes of transport became less acceptable.

Many rural Devon lines seem to have been built on the basis of 'there's a valley, quick build a railway up it'. In fact this simply reflected the physical difficulty of a county like Devon, dominated by the two massive hill systems of Exmoor and Dartmoor. Most set off to link the larger villages to the cities, driven by the need for local commerce to be connected to the main lines and thus to the rest of the country. This often resulted in junctions between the branch line and the main line that were, to all intents and purposes, miles from anywhere. What mattered though, was that there was now a link.

This might be a good point at which to explain the somewhat convoluted company structure involved in the early lines. The main line from London to Bristol had been built by the Great Western Railway Company and from the Midlands by the Gloucester and Bristol Railway Company. The section from Bristol to Exeter was the product of the Bristol and Exeter Railway Company, a somewhat truculent body that fell on difficult times and was later absorbed by the Great Western. The Exeter to Plymouth link was built by the South Devon Railway Company who also became part of the Great Western empire.

The other main line to venture into Devon was the London and South Western Railway Company who arrived in Exeter from London but via Salisbury and Honiton. After much manipulation they also reached Plymouth by going around Dartmoor to the north via Okehampton. They also eventually acquired the Exeter to Barnstaple line which meant that the connections between the three largest Devon towns and the rest of the country lay in the control of just two companies, the Great Western Railway (GWR) and the London & South Western Railway (LSWR).

Virtually every rural branch line, though usually built by small local companies, was dependant on the larger companies for their running and any through traffic they needed. This geographical stranglehold meant that it was almost inevitable that the smaller branch lines would, sooner or later, become part of these two big companies. In fact, in 1923, because of the sheer number of railway companies operating in Britain, the Government decided to force through what became known as 'Grouping'. This meant that every existing railway company had to join one of the four big companies, namely, the London, Midland & Scottish (LMS), the London and North Eastern Railway (LNER), the Southern Railway (SR) or the Great Western Railway (GWR). So, GWR, being one of these big four, continued to dominate the West Country right through to nationalisation in 1947, whilst the other major railway company in Devon became part of the newly-formed Southern Railway.

It is easy to look at the decline of the local branch lines with a shrug of the shoulders, as if they never were destined to do better, but that overlooks a hundred years of faithful and essential service to the rural communities. In the days before the car, the local country station was the centre of all commercial life with a quite extraordinary variety of goods being handled; none probably made the railway companies much profit but without them our country would now be a very different place.

Thanks to the restoration movement, two Devon lines were saved and today can be enjoyed behind steam engines once more, while smaller bands of enthusiasts are working on at least three other sites. Some of the old lines are now pathways and sometimes a former station site is being used by local industry – but the rest of Devon's railway heritage is, alas, rapidly disappearing beneath the plough or modern developments.

Stan Yorke

1
Plymouth South

The Lee Moor Tramway
Harbour branches
Turnchapel branch
Yealmpton branch

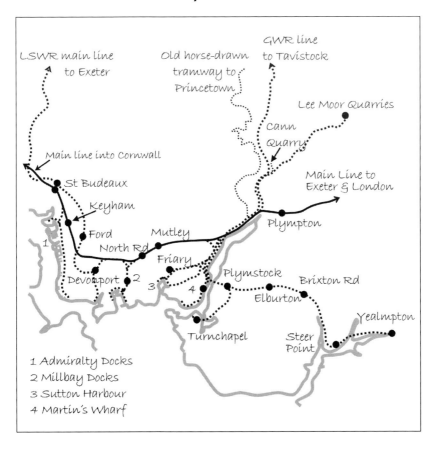

The Plymouth & Dartmoor Railway obtained its Act in 1821 and was opened to traffic two years later. Its 25½ miles of 4 ft 6 in gauge track originally ran from a riverside dock at Crabtree to the Foggintor Quarry high up on Dartmoor. Within two years, it was extended to the earliest commercial docks in Plymouth at Sutton Pool and as far north as Princetown, with the idea of regenerating the moorland town and its now disused 'Prison of War' by serving the local granite quarries. Much of its line followed the course of the Plymouth Leat, a waterway built by Sir Francis Drake to bring water down from near Yelverton to Plymouth. Branches were soon built to the Cann Quarry and to Plympton. Horse-drawn throughout its short life, it was abandoned in the 1840s but, as we shall see, much of the route was to be reused in later years.

The next line to enter Plymouth was the South Devon Railway which, with Brunel's guidance, had fought its way to Plymouth from Exeter. Built with broad gauge track (7 ft ¼ in) it arrived in 1848, and within a year had extended to a new terminus at Millbay. A further extension was soon built onwards from Millbay station to new docks that were later to grow into the Great Western Docks – the largest commercial docks in Plymouth. In 1851 another extension was built to Sutton Pool (soon to become Sutton Harbour), which followed the old Plymouth & Dartmoor tracks. In 1859, with the completion of Brunel's famous Saltash Bridge across the Tamar river, the Cornwall Railway entered Plymouth from the west and also used the Millbay station as its terminus.

The Lee Moor Tramway

This bold little horse-drawn 4 ft 6 in gauge line was built in 1855 (see Chapter 2) to bring china clay down from Lee Moor on the south-western edge of Dartmoor. There were eventually several such pits in the area covering some six square miles. China clay is a product of decomposed granite and is found in Cornwall (around St Austell) and at Lee Moor. It is washed out using water and the slurry that is produced is then dried. The prime

The lower end of the Cann incline showing how the lines opened up to provide separate lines for empty and full trains to be assembled. (Author's Collection)

Locomotive No 2 standing in its shed at Buckfastleigh along with superb maps and information sheets. (Author)

13

use is in the making of high-quality paper but it is also used in the production of porcelain, pharmaceuticals and cosmetics. Originally all the clay was dried adjacent to the pits at Lee Moor and brought down to the quayside in powder form by means of the tramway to be shipped to ports around the UK and also abroad.

The line started off from Lee Moor down a precipitous incline, which dropped 300 ft in a length of just 700 yds, and then continued downhill through the Cann woods and onto the second incline, which dropped the line a further 330 ft after which a short section took the line to a junction with the older

Just beyond the bottom of the Cann incline the tramway crossed over the GWR Plymouth–Tavistock branch . The infill between the rails was to aid the horses who worked the lower section. (Kidderminster Railway Museum)

The same spot today, with the tramway used as a pathway whilst the old GWR branch enters on the right and exits into the scrub on the left. (Author)

14

Virtually the only relic left in Plymouth, this Grade 2 listed bridge took the tramway across the river Plym before it turned south to disappear beneath the present day A38 interchange. (Author)

Cann Quarry line and thus into the valley of the river Plym and on into Plymouth. The section between the two inclines was later worked by a pair of locomotives. For the last mile or so, it left the old line and veered south to Martin's Wharf alongside the Plym, near Cattedown. The inclines, which accounted for 630 ft of the total climb of 740 ft, were worked by steel cables wound around drums at the top of the incline. The descending trucks were always heavier than the empties coming up so all that was needed was a braking system on the drums to control the speed. Both inclines had a passing place halfway along their length. The wharves expanded over the years when the LSWR built standard gauge lines to Cattewater in 1876 by which time the tramway had become almost buried in a maze of standard gauge tracks belonging to the GWR and the LSWR.

The output of the china clay works became more than the tramway could move and in 1927 the first pipeline was laid

A lovely shot of a 'train' approaching the crossing of the GWR main lines into Plymouth. It was usual to see a pair of horses pulling three or four wagons. (Author's Collection)

down to Marsh Mills to carry the clay in a liquid slurry to new works where the drying was carried out. It could then be taken by standard gauge GWR trains to Fowey in Cornwall which was the principal port handling china clay. Later still, it became more economic to pump all the china clay as slurry down to settling tanks rather than use the old railway and the last china clay traffic ran in 1945.

One novel feature was the crossing with the ever-expanding main lines at Laira Junction. The South Devon Railway on its approach to Plymouth had made provision for a crossing for the older Plymouth & Dartmoor Railway even though this was not in use at the time. When the Lee Moor Tramway used the old line it inherited the crossing and as the main lines grew in number the crossing for the little horse-drawn tramway was rebuilt and maintained.

After 1945 the line was retained but not worked, and groups of slowly rotting trucks could be found at several points along the route. In order to maintain a right of way, the clay company

16

One of the tramway slate rock sleeper blocks that can still be found along the route. (Author)

ran an occasional horse-drawn, two wagon train to convey sand from a loading ramp on a siding at Marsh Mills to Maddocks Concrete Works, which involved crossing the GWR main lines. Having finally decided to abandon the line, the last horse-drawn sand train, with just one wagon, plodded its way to the concrete works on 26th August 1960. Within months the main line level crossing was removed and, with the remaining track and trucks lifted, a second pipeline was laid on the old trackbed. By the following year virtually everything had been scrapped except for the two locomotives used on the middle section, one of which (No 2) went to the local Lee Moor Museum at Saltram House, Plympton and the other (No 1) to the Wheal Martyn China Clay Museum in Cornwall. The first locomotive (No 2) was recently moved to its own shed at the Buckfastleigh station of the South Devon Railway.

Traces of these two early systems can still be found, among them the trackbed, the long empty leat and the occasional milestone.

Harbour branches

To complete the early developments in Plymouth we must now add the London & South Western Railway (LSWR) lines. The LSWR arrived in 1865 by sharing the GWR line from Lydford to

Plymouth via Tavistock. It ran over the GWR lines through Plymouth, leaving at Devonport Junction, and then to its own terminus at Devonport. It later gained an independent route into Devonport in 1880 (as described in Chapter 5) and in order to reach Plymouth town (as opposed to the Devonport area) it built a new terminus at Plymouth Friary, which was reached by sharing the GWR line from Devonport Junction.

The largest dock system was the Admiralty Docks (Devonport), which surprisingly were fed by just one link to the GWR main line – a 1 in 70 climb laid down in 1867 to Keyham Junction. The dock system was vast, spreading for nearly 1½ miles along the Tamar estuary, with its own tramway, which was laid in the 1860s. Lines reached virtually every dock or berth. Alas, its military function prevented unofficial photographs being taken. It is hard to grasp just how big Devonport docks were, it was in effect a small city. Every kind of skill was present: there was a foundry plus machine shops, carpenters and all the facilities needed to service large war ships, as well as barracks, a parade ground and all the rest of the logistics catering for an ever-changing population. Within the docks there was also a passenger service, including two tunnels and six stations, which ran into the 1960s carrying both staff and naval personnel. The train consisted of four or five wooden coaches mounted on a secondhand goods truck chassis and ran a half-hourly service on weekdays. To cope with the wide variations in rank, the coaches provided no less than five classes.

The rail network continued in use for goods up to 1982 after which it slowly shrank until recent years when the docks became a commercial venture.

The commercial docks were based around the Great Western Docks (Millbay Docks), fed via the Millbay station lines, and the much more fragmented wharves around Sutton Harbour and the Plym estuary.

The large and businesslike Millbay Docks consisted of an inner (tide-free) basin and a larger outer basin. The inner basin was surrounded by warehouses, a small shipbuilding yard and a large graving (dry) dock. The outer basin held more warehouses, a timber yard and three piers that handled

A typical GWR dock engine that would have been found throughout the dock system. This restored loco originally worked in the South Wales docks. (Author)

passenger traffic. Much of this was the small tenders used to take passengers out to larger ocean-going ships which dropped anchor in Plymouth Sound. Passengers travelling to London could save a full day by disembarking here and completing their journey by rail. For the same reason vast quantities of mail were also handled, peaking in 1949 with over 430,000 bags, that's over 1,100 bags a day. In the days before motorways and airborne goods transport, vast amounts of goods moved through docks like Plymouth both from abroad and from around the UK.

One quaint little line was built by the LSWR railway from the goods yard of its Devonport station down to Stonehouse Pool where it fed a range of quays set around a half circle. It was used for boat trains from London to access the Ocean Quay station but this romantic service only ran from 1904 to 1911. The line finally closed in 1970, with part of the route becoming a footpath.

Sutton Pool, later promoted to Sutton Harbour, was the original starting point of the Plymouth and Dartmoor Railway back in 1823. In 1892 the GWR added a second branch to serve the north side of the pool. Later a short branch was added by the LSWR from the goods yard of its Friary station, dropping down to join the GWR lines and the north quays. These smaller harbours could handle traffic using coasters rather than the larger long-distance cargo ships that plied the oceans and, again in pre-motorway days, it is surprising just how much moved this way, including coal and timber. The goods traffic around the eastern side of Plymouth was often handled by the little ex LSWR B4 class 0-4-0 tank engines.

Turnchapel branch

This short branch was built by the LSWR, first reaching Plymstock in 1892 and eventually Turnchapel in 1897. The service used the LSWR terminus at Plymouth Friary and the

Plymouth Friary station with a Turnchapel train just setting off behind a LSWR '02' class 0-4-4 loco. This station was built by the LSWR to gain access to central Plymouth. (Kidderminster Railway Museum)

An enthusiasts' trip along the Turnchapel branch in 1959. Above in Plymstock station and below in Turnchapel. (J. H. Ashton)

The bridge that carried the line across the Plym river into Plymstock. The abutment of the old road bridge can be seen on the far bank just to the right of the rail bridge. (Author)

traffic rose from a modest eight trains per day at the start to a remarkable 26 a day in 1930, the journey taking just ten minutes to complete. There were two substantial bridges, the first (Laira Bridge), shared with the Yealmpton branch, was over the river Plym, the second was a swing bridge over Hooe Lake just before Turnchapel station. This bridge, around 100 ft long, was hand cranked by the signalman who must have been glad that it was rarely used. Turnchapel station was in a very strange position, being next to a large oil depot (destroyed in the 1940 hostilities) but still some 500 yards from the village. As with all Plymouth lines there were branches and spurs that fed wharves and factories. Just before the swing bridge a branch served a large timber and creosoting works, which remained working along with the rest of the line until 1961. The line also extended beyond

22

Turnchapel station, tunnelled under part of the village and fed into yet more Admiralty wharves.

From around 1905 a railmotor service ran and, later, O2 class 0-4-4 tank engines worked push-pull sets until the end in 1951. The goods service ended ten years later. There is a story of a passing local enthusiast who saw men with cutting gear starting to dismantle the Laira bridge; he rushed to stop them, pointing out that the bridge carried a large gas main! Work promptly halted and the bridge stands to this day, complete with its isolated track and gas pipe.

Yealmpton branch

This was originally promoted by the LSWR using the old Plymouth & Dartmoor Railway Acts, but the possibility of the LSWR extending towards the Torbay area so alarmed the GWR that the branch to Yealmpton was transferred to the GWR who opened it in 1898. In the first few years there were rumblings of other lines in the area, the first being the idea of completing the original Plymouth & Dartmoor plan to reach Modbury via Yealmpton. Oddly enough this section would have remained with the LSWR in an attempt to stop one company from sneaking into the territory of the other. Another proposal was for a light railway to be constructed from the line a mile or so short of Yealmpton, which would then follow the eastern edge of the river Yealm to reach Newton Ferrers. In fact Yealmpton station was built in Torr, on the 'wrong' side of the river for the real Yealmpton village, and the only road bridge over the river soon proved too narrow and was rebuilt.

Traffic grew steadily with a surprisingly varied selection of goods traffic, including milk, rabbits, animal feeds, oysters and bricks from the South Hams works near Steer Point. There was so much milk traffic that it was common for the luggage compartments to be full of it and churns were even lined up in the centre aisles of the passenger carriages. The first station on the branch, Billacombe, added lime and quarry stone to the mix. By the early 1920s the motor car was eating into the passenger

Elburton station with a hopeful passenger or two as the train for Plymouth approaches in 1942. (Lens of Sutton Association)

Steer Point station in its lonely setting by South Creek with a steam railcar arriving around 1912. (Lens of Sutton Association)

Yealmpton station with a push-pull train arriving from Plymouth around 1920. The passing loop was nearly twice the length of the station, possibly hoping for the extension that never came. (Lens of Sutton Association)

traffic and in 1928 the GWR announced that it was considering closure. With no improvement in the usage, passenger traffic ceased in 1930. Goods services continued but the stations and signalling were all stripped to the minimum. Three of the station buildings were converted to private dwellings, with fencing to separate them from the still active track and goods facilities. At Yealmpton, the base of the demolished signal box became an outhouse and later a chicken house. By 1941, with the Second World War under way, petrol had become very scarce and cars disappeared from the streets; even bus services were badly hit. The GWR therefore decided to reinstate the passenger services, and this involved hasty reconstruction of ticket offices and toilets at Yealmpton. Much traffic was generated by the demand to move people out of Plymouth during the heavy night-time bombing. Like many front-line towns, people in Plymouth, who had relations or friends who could take them in at night, left by train each evening for the safer outer suburbs or nearby villages.

To reopen a line just for this traffic was unusual and though the worst of the bombing had ended by 1943 the service to Yealmpton was maintained until 1947.

The branch left the Turnchapel route at Plymstock station, which had the odd feature of one platform serving LSWR (later Southern Railway) trains to Turnchapel and another platform serving the GWR trains to Yealmpton. The pre 1930 trains ran to and from the GWR Millbay station but the 1941 to 1947 services used the Southern Railway Friary station, albeit with GWR engines and coaches. There was also a GWR service from Plymstock through to Saltash using railmotors. The line was always purely rural with all stations having just one platform and a minimum of facilities.

The end of the war saw a slow but steady return to road transport and yet again passenger services ceased in 1947. By 1950 the goods traffic justified only one train a day and by 1958 the total of 4,500 tons of freight, mostly coal, needed just three trains a week. Freight services ended in 1960. As with many of Devon's condemned branch lines, a flutter of enthusiasts' trains came to visit. A short section at the Plymstock end was redeveloped for the nearby cement works and a new LPG gasworks but everything else was slowly removed and either went back to nature or was built over. Yealmpton station was demolished in 1971 and is now a small housing estate.

2
Plymouth North

Plymouth, Tavistock & Launceston Railway
Yelverton to Princetown

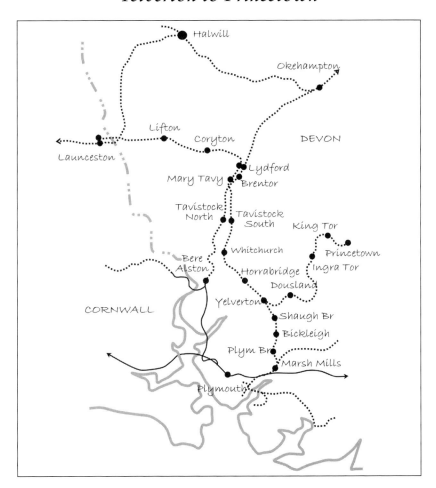

Plymouth, Tavistock & Launceston Railway

The early history of this line is an incredible saga of proposals and counter proposals and, in particular, it was plagued by that old red herring – the broad gauge. The Plymouth & Dartmoor Railway, which we have already met, was opened in 1823 and was a meandering horse-drawn line from the old Sutton Pool in Plymouth to Dartmoor, where the old prison was being restored. Though the ends of this line were built over by later lines, the centre section faded back into the scenery in the mid 1800s. The Lee Moor Tramway, again horse-drawn, did at least continue working until 1945 after which the china clay slurry was piped down to Plymouth.

The main line from Exeter into Cornwall is, of course, still busy with modern trains though the many sidings and goods yards around the Plymouth area have long vanished.

The section to Tavistock was built by the South Devon & Tavistock Railway Company under the leadership of Lord Morley. Originally the company was involved in building the Lee Moor Tramway, which was complete by 1855 but was found to be of a very poor standard. The company wisely disposed of this line and returned to the job in hand of reaching Tavistock, which they achieved in 1859. During this time an additional bill was passed whereby the line would be leased to the South Devon Railway Company who would be operating the new line in any case. The original engineer, A. H. Bampton, had died early on in the construction and Brunel took on the job but, in practice, the supervision was provided by Brunel's assistant, Mr Brereton. The line, built to the broad gauge, left the South Devon main line and headed north, following the Lee Moor Tramway up the river Plym valley for about 1½ miles to where the tramway crossed the line on a level crossing and headed off towards the quarries. The Lee Moor Tramway was, in fact, a branch of the older Cann Quarry line and the new line passed under and then over this in the next half mile. This first mile or so was further complicated by the remains of the older Cann

28

Marsh Mills station as it is today, the centre of the Plym Valley Railway. Track and steam train services are being extended towards the old Lee Moor Tramway crossing to provide the sound and smell of steam once again in the Plym valley. (Author)

Plym Bridge Platform just one stop further on but the line is now starting to climb in earnest. (Lens of Sutton Association)

By Ham Viaduct, north of Bickleigh, the line was well above the valley floor and viaducts were needed to cross several side valleys. (Author)

The next stop is the little Shaugh Bridge Platform. There is no trace of the original broad gauge or the dual gauge days. (Lens of Sutton Association)

Canal whose remains intertwined the railways plus, of course, the ever-present river. From here the line continued on its own up the valley along the river Meavy to Yelverton. One tunnel had been needed at Shaugh, with a second at Yelverton (there was no station here until 1885). Continuing in a generally northward direction, the line passed Horrabridge, went through a third short tunnel at Grenofen and so arrived at Tavistock.

Several viaducts had been needed, as one would expect from the difficult terrain. Originally constructed of wood on top of masonry pillars they were rebuilt between 1893 and 1910 in brick or granite; the largest, at Walkham, was 367 yds long and 132 ft high. The line climbed at a fairly hard gradient of around 1 in 60 to Yelverton and then descended at a similar rate towards Tavistock.

Though the people of Plymouth had been somewhat indifferent to the project, the good folk of Tavistock were jubilant. The line was single throughout except for passing loops

Yelverton station where the Princetown branch started (on the left). An auto train has arrived from Plymouth on its way to Tavistock in the late 1910s. (Lens of Sutton Association)

Horrabridge station where the Princetown train originally started from in 1912. The space between the tracks shows the broad gauge origins. (Lens of Sutton Association)

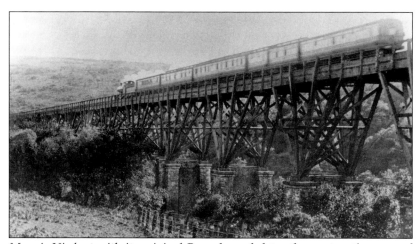

Magpie Viaduct with its original Brunel wooded trestle construction around 1910, prior to reconstruction. Like all the trestle bridges this was rebuilt in brick. (Lens of Sutton Association)

Whitchurch Down, the last station before Tavistock. Though now dropping at a good rate, the need for viaducts and tunnels is past. (Lens of Sutton Association)

at Bickleigh, Yelverton and Horrabridge. A service of five trains was provided with four on Sundays but this was quickly reduced to two. The line was an immediate success with goods traffic building up quickly. There was copper ore traffic at Horrabridge and Crelake and lime and coal traffic to Yelverton and Tavistock. As had been expected the company became amalgamated with the South Devon Railway Company in 1865.

A station was opened at Marsh Mills in 1860 and this area provided yet more goods traffic. Firstly a flour mill opened then the Dartmoor China Clay Company built settling tanks that dried the slurry and left the resultant powder to be taken by rail to Fowey harbour in Cornwall. In 1932 a tarmac works joined the array of sidings. Road stone was also brought down from near Tavistock in considerable quantities until 1952.

The wooden station in Tavistock burnt down in 1887 and was rebuilt in stone and, in common, with many GWR West Country stations, it had an all-over roof.

Tavistock South, with its typical GWR overall roof, was the main station on the line. Today the site is home to the fire station and ambulance depot plus a development of retirement homes. (Lens of Sutton Association)

Launceston was something of a lost cause in the early 1800s; it had been reduced to having a single Member of Parliament, the Assizes had transferred to Bodmin along with the gaol and its somewhat battered population started to disperse. Nevertheless, it had tried again and again to get a railway connection, preferably via Okehampton to Exeter, but by the 1850s it was happy to be connected to almost anywhere! After the usual wrangles with landowners the line onwards to Launceston was built by the Launceston & South Devon Railway Company and opened in 1865. Built in broad gauge it made an end-on connection at Tavistock. The line was immediately successful, with over 19,000 passengers carried in the first year, along with nearly 19,000 tons of goods. The company was amalgamated with the South Devon Railway in 1873 and, along with all the South Devon lines, became part of the Great Western Railway in 1878.

The line set off in a northerly direction from Tavistock,

climbing to its summit at Lydford (originally Lidford) some 650 ft above sea level. Well, at least near to Lydford, which was actually some 1½ miles further north. It now turned sharply west into the Lyd valley, through Lifton and into the valley of the Tamar and so into Launceston where it entered its terminus. Gradients were still fairly steep with sections of 1 in 63, 1 in 55 and 1 in 40 and banking engines were used on the heavier freight trains.

Once the railway arrived, Launceston grew from strength to strength though there were still complaints about the somewhat miserly service of only 3 trains a day to Plymouth. As we shall see in Chapter 6 the arrival in 1886 of a second standard gauge line in the town at last realised the hope of a direct route to Exeter.

For some years Coryton station handled large quantities of manganese, reaching 4,000 tons in 1872. The early traffic gave rise to numerous calls for more sidings and better facilities. One long-standing cry was for a station at the junction in Plymouth,

Lydford station showing the GWR line just before it turns west to head down the Lyd valley. The LSWR lines are to the right of the picture, which was taken in the 1960s. (Lens of Sutton Association)

Lifton station and just to the left the Ambrosia dairy which expanded after the line closed, covering both the station and the land towards the camera. (Lens of Sutton Association)

where the Tavistock line left the main line to Exeter, to save passengers from having to go right into Plymouth to change trains. As early as 1861 there had been a request for a station at Shaugh to serve the Dewerstone area which was eventually built - in 1907! Lifton saw more agricultural produce, including grain for the local mills, and dealt with a flourishing trade in milk destined for London. Launceston itself produced significant quantities of goods traffic, including livestock. The station had a goods shed, engine shed, water crane and a turntable plus sidings. The name was later changed to Launceston North in 1951 but it closed in 1952 with the Tavistock trains using the ex-LSWR station instead.

The LSWR was to disturb the peace of our line in a more dramatic way. The LSWR-backed Devon and Cornwall Railway Company had reached Lydford in 1874 with its standard gauge line. The relevant Act allowed for its trains to use the Plymouth to Tavistock line to gain access into Plymouth and so in 1876 our broad gauge line had a third rail added to permit this. The line now ran as a dual gauge, two-company railway until 1890 when a separate standard gauge line was built from Lydford to Plymouth. The link between the two lines was removed and they operated separately until the link was replaced in 1943 as a wartime measure. This gave rise at the Lee Moor crossing to three gauges in one spot, the 4 ft 6 in of the Lee Moor line, the 7 ft ¼ in broad gauge and the 4 ft 8½ in standard gauge.

In 1922, just a mile or so north of Tavistock, sidings were put in to serve the Pitt's Cleave Quarry which supplied road stone and ballast for the GWR.

Early locomotives on the line were mostly 4-4-0 saddle tanks joined by 0-6-0 tank engines used on freight workings. Following conversion to standard gauge in 1892 various Dean 3500 class engines worked the line and later the 4500 class tank engines took over and stayed right to the end. Steam railmotors and later auto trains took over much of the passenger services in the early 1900s and a sprinkling of pannier tanks lasted throughout. During the 1900s there was a good service to Tavistock of around ten to fourteen trains on weekdays, though Launceston saw only four or five.

The end came, as so often, as a series of economy measures starting with the closure of the terminus at Launceston, trains being diverted into the ex-LSWR station from 1952. The tarmac works at Marsh Mills closed the same year. In 1955 the Lee Moor Tramway finally gave up and the level crossings were removed, to be followed a year later by the closure of the Princetown branch from Yelverton. This robbed the southern end of the line of both passenger and freight traffic, each loss edging the line towards being uneconomical. In 1959 Bickleigh station lost its signal box and passing loop. Passenger services ended in 1962, with freight services lingering on around Lydford until 1966. The last passenger trains were caught in dreadful weather with passengers stranded in snow-blocked stations and, despite gallant efforts by the staff, the very last scheduled train couldn't run.

The track was promptly lifted and most of the stations soon

disappeared, either under grass and scrub or under factories. Today, a short section in the Plym valley has been restored as the Plym Valley Railway, working north from Marsh Mills.

Yelverton to Princetown

We have already mentioned the early 4 ft 6 in gauge horse-drawn Plymouth & Dartmoor Railway, which wound its tortuous route from Plymouth through what was to become Yelverton and up to Princetown. Though originally built to take materials up to Princetown to build the prison, this line depended for traffic on the granite quarried at Ingra Tor, Swell Tor and Foggintor but by the late 1840s this trade had declined, leaving Princetown devoid of work and wealth. The prison of war had been closed around 1820, following peace treaties with France and America. In 1850 the prison was reopened as a

A view of the Yelverton junction looking towards the Princetown line in the late 1910s. At the end of the platform the line started climbing hard with little rest until Princetown was reached. (Lens of Sutton Association)

38

A train steadily climbing near Dousland in 1949. Alas, the single coach was usually all that was needed. (Kidderminster Railway Museum)

conventional establishment and some prosperity returned to Princetown. Though the line was unused, the company, dominated by the Johnson Brothers who owned the quarries, was still very much alive. Following several abandoned attempts to build a line to Princetown, the Johnson Brothers suggested in 1877 that they sell the Yelverton to Princetown section of the old horse-drawn line to a new company to be called the Princetown Railway Company. Jointly owned by the GWR and the Johnsons, the line was opened in 1883. Laid in standard gauge it joined the Plymouth to Tavistock line at Yelverton, which at the time still didn't have a station, the service running to and from Horrabridge. Two years later a junction station was built at Yelverton and the Princetown trains operated from here for the rest of the line's life. In 1922 the company was absorbed into the GWR.

The line left Yelverton on a sharp curve, which continued on

Princetown station showing the modest sidings and engine shed. The turntable was just out of the picture to the right. (Kidderminster Railway Museum)

The scene today. Only the houses on the left give a clue to where the station was. (Author)

an embankment rising at 1 in 40 as it turned from facing south to facing north. A cutting followed, which brought the new line onto the old Plymouth and Dartmoor trackbed. Soon Dousland station was reached after which the route was totally dependent on the contours of the massive Dartmoor hills. Over the next seven miles the direction would change seven times before heading along the final two miles into Princetown, with just Ingra Tor halt and King Tor halt for company. The maximum gradient was around 1 in 40, which occurred throughout the journey climbing towards Princetown except for one short half-mile section of downhill at 1 in 41. The line rose 895 ft in its 10½ miles. The speed throughout was limited to 20 mph. The new station was not quite as far into Princetown as the original and was furnished with a loop, a siding, a goods shed, an engine shed and a small turntable. For most of its life there were four or five trains each day, with a peak of seven during the early 1910s. The Sunday service was just two trains but it didn't run for many years. The summer months produced a good deal of tourist traffic but the quarry traffic ended in the late 1930s and the line saw a steady decline after the war, eventually closing in 1956.

Originally powered by small 0-6-0 tank engines of the 517 and 1901 classes the line became home from 1905 to Churchward's 4400 class small 2-6-2 tanks. For the last couple of years the 4500 class locomotives took over. The weather in winter was always difficult and indeed was used as an argument for the rescuing of the line but in the 1950s saving uneconomical lines was seen as a social issue and thus of no concern to the Ministry of Transport.

3
Branches South of Dartmoor

Totnes to Ashburton
Newton Abbot to Moretonhampstead
Heathfield to Exeter – the Teign Valley Railway

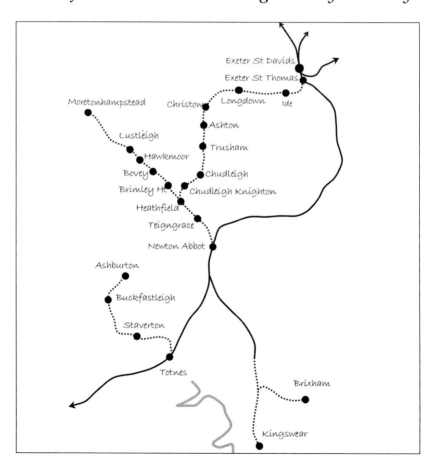

Totnes to Ashburton

The Ashburton area of Devon was once an important centre for the wool trade and this had led to proposals for a railway connection as soon as the South Devon Railway was opened but nothing happened until 1863 when the Buckfastleigh, Totnes & South Devon Railway was incorporated. Powers to extend to Ashburton came the following year and the line was opened in 1872. Built in the broad gauge it was operated by the South Devon Railway until 1875 and then by the GWR. The company was absorbed into the GWR in 1897, five years after the track was changed to the standard gauge. Even though the wool trade was now declining, Buckfastleigh still provided more traffic in 1890 than even Newton Abbot.

The line followed the valley of the river Dart, climbing steadily and reaching Buckfastleigh with only one short section of 1 in 50. The ascent to Ashburton was steeper with three sections that were around 1 in 60 and used the valley of the minor river Ashburn. In true Devonian style the stations for

Classic rural Devon scene with engine no 1472 and a single coach near Buckfastleigh in 1958. (Kidderminster Railway Museum)

43

Buckfastleigh station in 1955 with regular engine, 1400 class 0-4-2T No 1470. (Kidderminster Railway Museum)

The scene today, the headquarters of the South Devon Railway, which goes to great lengths to recreate the atmosphere of the rural line. (Author)

Staverton and Buckfastleigh were both around a mile from their respective villages though Ashburton station was only a short walk from the village centre. Originally only Ashburton had an engine shed and turntable though this last item was only used until around the early 1900s.

The passenger services started around the four trains a day level and, give or take a few ups and downs, rose steadily until some eight trains ran each way in the 1950s. The Sunday service was always poor or non-existent. The track layout at Totnes, where the branch line started, was dreadful. Not only was there no bay to handle the branch line traffic, but the feed to the goods shed left the down platform line immediately at the end of the

44

Ashburton terminus in 1957 complete with cattle pens and gas works. (Lens of Sutton Association)

platform. This meant that branch line trains had to fit in between both stopping and through trains on the main line – wave goodbye to any good connecting services – plus any shunting of goods wagons to or from the goods shed virtually closed half the station. As with most of the South Devon GWR-operated branch lines, the locomotives were normally 0-4-2 tanks of the 517, 1400 or 4800 classes, originally with four-wheeled coaches. After the 1920s auto trains were used. There was a daily goods train conveying the usual mixture of coal and rural products and the passenger services could normally be handled by a single coach.

During the first half of the 20th century, the line became the archetypal Great Western rural branch much loved by railway buffs and modellers, but its meagre traffic after the Second World War couldn't maintain the line and it closed to passengers in 1958 with goods traffic ending in 1962.

Restoration

After long negotiations, the Dart Valley Light Railway Company took over the line as far as Buckfastleigh. It had hoped to reach Ashburton and initially leased this section of the line allowing

45

Today beautifully restored ex GWR locomotives work the line. No 5526 is just leaving Staverton station en route to Totnes Littlehempston. (Author)

Staverton platform, and yes it really is the 21st century! (Author)

much work to be put in to restore the station but the fickle Devon County Council who opposed the original closure now opposed the reopening! You won't, however, be surprised to hear that the Buckfastleigh to Ashburton section became swallowed up in the A38 road improvements soon after. Today, the line from Buckfastleigh, now known as the South Devon Railway, still runs steam-hauled trains though it is no longer allowed to enter Totnes station on the main line but instead has built its own terminus, which is a short walk away. This was known as Totnes Riverside but following splendid work by volunteers who built a complete station (mostly from parts of closed Somerset or Dorset stations) it is now called Totnes Littlehempston.

Tracing the only really 'lost' section of the line is very difficult owing to the almost complete decimation of the line by the A38 improvements but a few remains can be identified within Ashburton, including the old goods shed.

Newton Abbot to Moretonhampstead

There had been several schemes suggested in the 1840s for lines that would have served the Bovey valley and

The branch train waiting to depart from its bay platform in Newton Abbot station in 1935. Judging by the positions of the driver and guard they are waiting for a late running main line connection from Plymouth. (Author's Collection)

Heathfield station in 1958 with a Teign Valley train waiting to depart. On the left is the siding into Candy's Brick and Tile works. (Kidderminster Railway Museum)

The same scene today with no trace of the siding though Candy's is still there. The Teign Valley branch has also completely disappeared under trees. (Author)

Moretonhampstead but nothing came of them until a committee of local landowners and businessmen was formed in 1858. These good men made somewhat slow progress but eventually in 1862 the Moretonhampstead & South Devon Railway received its Act. The southern part of the proposed line followed the old Stover Canal and part of the Haytor Granite Tramway, both owned by the Duke of Somerset who insisted that the new company should purchase them outright. As with so many rural lines in Devon the company now found that enthusiasm rarely translated into money! After several behind the scenes meetings, the South Devon Railway Company agreed that it would support the new line and indeed supply a large part of the building costs. So construction began and following two years of financial juggling the line finally opened in 1866 as a broad gauge line, climbing 550 ft in its 12-mile journey from Newton Abbot.

The Granite Tramway was provided with an exchange siding and a crane and a separate siding was built to serve the Bovey Pottery, both in 1867. The early years proved difficult, to say the least, and in 1872 the company was amalgamated with the South Devon Railway Company. Just four years later the South Devon was absorbed into the Great Western Railway and so our line became yet another GWR branch line. The original pattern of four trains continued with a goods service as far as Bovey, goods

Bovey Tracey in 1959, always a well-kept station with flower beds and hanging baskets in summer. (Kidderminster Railway Museum)

Today the Bovey bypass has taken over the trackbed but the little station building survives as a local heritage centre. (Author)

49

Lustleigh station in 1957 with 5500 class Pannier tank No 3600 pulling a very short goods train. (Lens of Sutton Association)

for Moretonhampstead being attached to passenger trains at Bovey. Rather oddly Bovey Tracey station was always known simply as Bovey. In 1882 the GWR added another train to the service and goods trains now ran the whole length of the line. In 1888 a siding was added at Heathfield to serve the Great Western Pottery, Brick and Tile Works owned by Candy & Co. In the late 19th century, sidings were put in south of Teigngrace to serve the local ball clay industry. Teigngrace station had in fact been built as a gesture to the Duke of Somerset who owned the nearby Stover House and who had sold the railway the land they needed. Part of this deal was that the Duke acquired the right to stop any train at Teigngrace that he wished to travel on! Along with all the remaining GWR broad gauge lines, it was converted to standard gauge in 1892.

Despite the early indifference from its masters, traffic increased around the turn of the century boosted by tourists from the Torbay area who flocked to the line for a trip into the beautiful outskirts of Dartmoor. By 1911 the service had

Moretonhampstead station with a two-coach auto train in the 1930s. The site is now a small industrial estate though some of the old station buildings can still be recognised. (Lens of Sutton Association)

increased to 8 trains a day, more on Wednesdays and Saturdays. Goods traffic, particularly coal, remained steady but only enough to justify one train a day until the 1940s. During the 1920s the tourist traffic was boosted by through trains from Paignton and Torquay. These were met at Bovey and Moreton by AEC charabancs, which took visitors on moorland tours to see the delights of Dartmoor and its more remote villages. Services peaked in the mid 1930s, with eleven trains, of which seven were through trains from the Torbay area, plus a further seven trains travelling just to Bovey. Like the Teign Valley line described in the next section, the line originally used small tank engines and four-wheeled or six-wheeled coaches followed by auto trains. It never saw DMUs nor was there ever any real attempt to face up to the road competition.

Everywhere, however, there were signs of cars, lorries and buses and nobody could have been in any doubt that the future for these small rural lines was in danger. Apart from a brief

51

burst of activity for the Royal Show in 1952, which was held at Stover Park, traffic faded away, partly due to deliberately inconvenient services, a trick used by British Rail to speed the end of many lines. Passenger services ended in 1959 and, despite a recommendation from the Central Transport Users Consultative Committee to reconsider the service using diesel railcars, nothing was done. A preservation society was formed with hopes of keeping the line alive but to no avail. The section beyond Bovey Tracey was closed in 1964 and, by 1971, all was inactive except the line from Newton Abbot to Heathfield. This was even used to stable the Royal Train in 1969 when the Queen reviewed the Fleet in Torbay. In 1987 the Bovey bypass, which used 1½ miles of the old trackbed, opened. A variety of goods traffic, including clay, oil and a short-lived banana ripening plant, kept the line to Heathfield open but by 1996 all such movement ceased. Only the ball clay traffic made it into the 21st century.

Heathfield to Exeter – the Teign Valley Railway

Plans for an inland route between Newton Abbot and Exeter had come and gone when finally in 1882 a line was opened from Heathfield, on the Moretonhampstead line, to Ashton with a siding that extended to Teign House (later to become the site of Christow station). This short standard gauge line had needed 9 Acts of Parliament to conquer the 7 miles! Like so many of the lines described in this book, its birth was slow and painful. A Mr William Toogood – a solicitor and, for a while, manager and secretary of the embryo company – was in dispute over money allegedly owed to him whilst the company was in no way satisfied with his explanation of its finances. Creditors were pressing and indeed the poor company was saved only by the chairman, Lord Haldon, taking over its property plus a mortgage on the lands. Further works to meet the requirements of the GWR, who were to work the line,

Heathfield station in 1920 with the Teign Valley train about to leave from the bay platform behind a 4400 class 2-6-2 locomotive. The train on the left is the 'main line' to Moretonhampstead. (Lens of Sutton Association)

Chudleigh station around 1910, with a 517 class, 0-4-2 tank engine. This part of the line is now buried beneath the A38. (Lens of Sutton Association)

Trusham station, with possibly the same 517 class engine photographed in 1912. The smoke and steam in the distance are from the nearby granite quarries. (Lens of Sutton Association)

Restored 10 ton private owner wagon from the Teign Valley Granite Company whose quarries were just outside Trusham. (Author)

followed before public services could begin later in 1882. The line was somewhat isolated as the Moretonhampstead line was still broad gauge, so all traffic had to be reloaded at Heathfield.

A year later a second line, the Exeter, Teign Valley & Chagford Railway, was authorised to continue the branch the 10 miles to reach Exeter but despite an enthusiastic launch the money simply didn't come in. This proposal also included a branch to Chagford, a journey of some 10 miles, which passed virtually no other settlement on the way. Bearing in mind that Chagford is only 4 miles from Moretonhampstead from where the GWR already operated a bus service, there seems very little to commend the extension.

In 1894 a new prospectus was launched for the Exeter & Teign Valley Railway Company and this time the promise of money was forthcoming. Work began promptly and soon many of the deep cuttings had been dug, as had the two tunnels at Culver and Perridge. There is a delightful record of the final blasting on these two tunnels where local dignitaries and their wives and daughters were invited to fire the final four or five blasts to complete the breakthrough. Even today it is a little hard to imagine fine ladies being keen to enter a tunnel in order to detonate dynamite! The section into Exeter was to prove a headache – the engineering was not the problem but landowners and reluctant shareholders were. The Ecclesiastical Commissioners and the Earl of Devon prevaricated over the purchase of the necessary land. But the inaccuracies of the prospectus caused the longest delays as calls for subscribed money failed to produce results.

Eventually, though, the line was completed in 1903. Built as a single, standard gauge line it made an end-on junction with the Teign Valley line at Christow. This in turn now enjoyed through working onto the Moretonhampstead line, which had been converted to standard gauge in 1892.

The chance of greater fame flickered in 1898 when plans were drawn up for a line from the Teign Valley branch to Ashburton and on to Brent on the existing main line to Plymouth. Had this ever been built it would have provided the shortest route from

55

Exeter to Plymouth with far less arduous gradients than the original main line.

The line had eight stations, serving Chudleigh Knighton, Chudleigh, Trusham, Ashton, Christow, Dunsford Halt, Longdown (the summit) and Ide. Trusham was the most important station, due to the amount of goods traffic generated by the local quarries and concrete works. There were various other quarries in the Ashton and Christow area all providing traffic, much of which continued into the 1950s.

There were two quarries at Trusham, the rock being removed by hand or steam drills, sometimes aided by dynamite. It was then conveyed to steam-driven crushers which reduced the size to suit the customer's needs before being loaded into railway wagons. Many of the earlier services worked to and from the Exeter St Thomas station, which was situated nearly a mile south of the main St Davids station but, in later years, all trains used St Davids, stopping at St Thomas on route. The line also had connections to sidings and the short branch that served the canal basin in Exeter.

Worked by the GWR it enjoyed good traffic levels until the

Christow station was the original terminus, seen here in the early 1930s. (Lens of Sutton Association)

Longdown station, the summit of the line. The station was at the end of a narrow, steep lane a mile or so from the village. Passengers consisted of a few commuters to Exeter and some of the local school children. The most important function was receiving coal for the local 'big' house. (Lens of Sutton Association)

1940s, including being used when bad weather closed the shore line through Dawlish. Trains like the Cornish Riviera were slowly drawn along the line by two engines, plus a banking engine, until they regained the main line at Newton Abbot, as were a considerable number of through goods trains considered too important to be delayed by the Dawlish weather problems. Having been built so late in the traditional railway era, the line was served by fairly modern locomotives (GWR class 517 and later 14XX). Steam railcars were used in the 1920s and push-pull auto trains ran for many years. Class 4500, 5100, 5300, 5500 and 5700 engines all saw employment, though no British Railways designed locomotives. Coaches were a motley mixture of four-wheel and six-wheel early GWR types with later bogie coaches arriving in the 1930s, but DMUs were never used on the line.

The passenger services peaked in the 1930s with nine trains

A Teign Valley train setting off from Exeter St Davids. It will shortly stop at the St Thomas station before turning west to climb the lonely hills to Longdown. (Millbrook House)

each way though there appears to have been no service on Sundays. Despite advertising the Moretonhampstead line for tourism, the Teign Valley was never promoted and the traffic gradually declined to five trains a day in the 1950s. The emergency use ended after nationalisation when the Southern Railway's line via Okehampton became the alternative route if the Dawlish line was closed. In 1957 a new timetable was introduced along with several cost saving measures, all of which could have been made earlier had the interest existed. This was, as usual, a burst of activity to permit British Rail to say that they tried all they could before applying for closure. The line was closed between Exeter and Christow in 1958. Goods traffic continued from Heathfield to Christow until floods damaged the track in 1960, leaving the line cut back to the Trusham cement works. All traffic ended in 1967 after which the Chudleigh Knighton to Chudleigh section vanished beneath yet more A38 trunk road improvements.

4
To the Seaside by the Great Western Railway

Paignton to Kingswear
Churston to Brixham
Brent to Kingsbridge – the Primrose Line

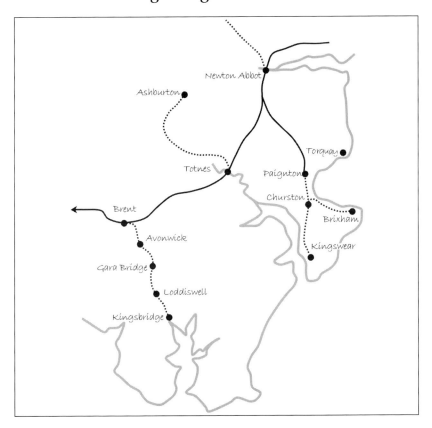

Paignton to Kingswear

The story of this line is relatively straightforward but it does encapsulate the notion that the earlier the railway was built, the more likely was its route to be viable. The South Devon Railway had opened its line from Exeter to Newton Abbot in 1846 as the first part of its drive to Plymouth. Just the next year it obtained an Act to build an extension to Torquay and one year later the line opened, the terminus being the present-day station of Torre. The line was now extended three times and the dates are interesting – one gets the clear impression of less and less commercial pressure as the intended targets got smaller and the risk greater.

The Dartmouth & Torbay Railway Company obtained an Act to complete the route in 1857 and the next section to Paignton opened in 1859; that's already eleven years after reaching Torre. The next section to Churston, then called Brixham Road, opened in 1861, with the final push to Kingswear being completed by

In 1961 a type 4 diesel hydraulic locomotive 'Strongbow' hauls the Torbay Express up the climb to Churston with Torbay in the background. (Kidderminster Railway Museum)

Churston station on a busy Saturday in 1957. Just disappearing under the footbridge is a train to Kingswear whilst a double headed train for Liverpool prepares to leave on the right. The Brixham branch train waits in the bay on the left. (Kidderminster Railway Museum)

1864 – some sixteen years to complete the ten miles from Torre, though in fairness the engineering gets much harder after Paignton. The original hopes had been to get the line to Dartmouth but this was thwarted by one of the landowners. In practice, crossing the Dart river valley would have been very expensive and I have doubts as to just how real the hopes were.

The line was built as a single broad gauge track and was operated by the South Devon Railway Company. It became part of the GWR in 1876 and was converted to standard gauge in 1892. The track to Kingskerswell was doubled in 1876, to Torquay in 1882, and to Paignton in 1910. This section is still operated by Rail Track, with a regular DMU service. South of Paignton, at Goodrington Sands, extensive sidings were built in the 1930s, which included a goods depot. Their main use, however, was as storage for the long sets of carriages that came to Torbay in the summer.

Kingswear station in 1946 with all the facilities in place. Note the turntable hiding just beneath the footbridge. Both locomotives are GWR 'Star' class with the usual four coach sets. (Kidderminster Railway Museum)

Passenger services had always been good, with eight trains to Kingswear in the first year of operation. This increased steadily until a peak in 1914 saw some 27 trains on weekdays and five on Sundays. Most local and out of season trains were worked by railmotors and later by auto trains. Substantial goods traffic existed, including coal for the Torbay gasworks. Prior to 1939 its coal was landed at Kingswear and brought up the line; later coal came direct from the pits, peaking in the 1950s at some 150 wagons per week. There were still nineteen trains running in 1955, with nine on Sundays but by 1969 this was down to twelve trains and no Sunday service. By 1971, all the Kingswear trains, bar just one through train, started from Paignton, involving a change of trains for through passengers.

Restoration
The section from Paignton falls into the 'almost lost' category. It was worked by steam engines until around 1961 when diesel

Churston today. The end of the old Brixham bay has been built over and new work sheds have been erected on the right but the station is still the same. (Author)

The same spot as the photo taken in 1961, but in 2006 with restored 2-6-2 locomotive No 4555 bringing its train up to Churston. (Author)

Kingswear in 2007 with No 4555 running around its train. Behind the rebuilt station roof is the ferry across to Dartmouth. (Author)

units took over – but the usual signs were around. The Brixham branch closed in 1963, goods traffic faded in the early 1960s and British Rail announced the closure for 1972. Luckily they had given plenty of notice and the Dart Valley Light Railway Company, whom we have already met in Chapter 3, were able to purchase the Paignton to Kingswear section in December 1972. At Paignton they took over five sidings that ran alongside the BR station. Two of these were kept as the platform and run round loop, whilst the other three were removed to make space for the steam railway's station and offices.

The Devon County Council subsidy for carrying school children soon lapsed and the line had to become seasonal in order to remain viable. It operated as the Torbay Steam Railway until 1976, as the Torbay & Dartmouth Railway until 1987 since when its title has became the Paignton & Dartmouth Steam Railway.

The preserved steam line received lots of work in the early years. Without space at Paignton the company developed Churston to become their engineering works. Kingswear was in a sorry state with all the sidings including the turntable having long gone. The Dart Valley Light Railway Company (now known as just the Dart Valley Railway) reinstated the bay platform and restored the classic GWR roof over the station tracks. It is very difficult to appreciate just how much work was done – today it all looks completely natural as if nothing has changed since the line was built.

Churston to Brixham

Brixham had been a busy port for many years; as early as the 1500s it had been the largest fishing port in the South West. By the start of the 1800s it was far larger than Torquay and Paignton together and, by 1830, some 1,000 men and boys worked in the fishing industry alone. It had its own shipbuilding industry and in 1842 iron oxide deposits were found nearby, adding yet more prosperity to the area, which was already described as the wealthiest place for its size on the south coast of England. The

The Brixham train departing from its bay at Churston in 1957 behind a 1400 class 0-4-2 engine, so beloved of smaller GWR branch lines. (Kidderminster Railway Museum)

original (1846) plans for the line to Kingswear included a branch to Brixham but this was curtailed, to just north of Torquay, by locals who objected to possibly losing their access to the beaches. By the time the line moved on through Torquay and Paignton the Brixham branch had disappeared from the agenda. When one considers how short the distance is, it is strange that the original South Devon Railway didn't include Brixham in its later works, indeed as its principal target.

After several attempts a local, and wealthy, solicitor with mining interests, R.W. Wolston, proposed a branch from the recently opened Brixham Road station on the Kingswear line to Brixham. He personally provided over £17,000 of the £18,000 capital and the Torbay & Brixham Railway duly obtained its Act in 1864. The original contractor, one Mr Jackson, defaulted before any work had been done and the intrepid Mr Wolston came to the rescue once again and took over the construction. After several minor problems were solved, the railway opened in 1868, with just one locomotive of its own plus carriages and wagons leased from the South Devon Railway Company.

It had been the project of virtually one man and, despite the local celebrations, there was an obvious lack of traffic and money. The little second-hand locomotive was mortgaged within six months of the opening, which did not bode well. The early years were financially bleak partly due to improper accounting by the South Devon Railway Company and Richard Wolston retired to Weston super Mare, a broken man and now declared insolvent. He had sold his mining interests in 1872. Throughout this rather sad state of affairs, the railway was carrying a steadily increasing number of passengers and a burgeoning amount of fish and general goods. Nevertheless, the disagreements with the South Devon continued and its behaviour seems to have been downright dishonest. Mainly as a result of two judgments against the South Devon, the Torbay & Brixham Railway was able to wrestle itself free of debt and became independent for the first time. New directors and management were able to increase revenue but no matter what they did, the fact that they were totally dependent on the South Devon Railway (later the GWR) for their link to the outside world via Churston, meant they were always doomed to an ignominious end. The line was purchased by the GWR in 1883 for just £12,000. The inconveniently placed station at Brixham had been tolerated as there was no alternative transport but, as soon as buses and cars arrived, local passengers left. Long-distance traffic like holidaymakers, coal and fish kept the line open; indeed, fish was carried nearly every day until the line's closure in 1963.

Along with all the remaining broad gauge lines in Devon, the branch had been changed over to standard gauge in 1892 and, as always, a fair number of trains continued to run each day. Connections at Churston were not always as good as they might have been. There is a lovely story of an old lady, nicknamed Mother Kennar by the station staff, who regularly went to the midweek market in Newton Abbot. She always arrived just at

Brixham station in 1962 just one year before final closure, the spread of sidings in good condition showing unfulfilled hopes. (Kidderminster Railway Museum)

the last minute and the staff became used to holding a door open for her – often the train, already under way, would stop again to allow her to board. On one occasion, it even reversed back into the station to allow her to get in!

Auto trains started in 1929 and the service now reached twenty trains each day. The local engine shed was soon closed, though, with the engine running down from Newton Abbot early in the morning and returning late at night. An idea of just how much traffic had been lost to the buses can be gauged from the seven days of the Devon General bus strike in 1957 when the railway carried over 15,000 passengers – more than the entire normal summer season.

Today little remains to be seen; the line had been constructed with a minimum of heavy engineering in order to contain the cost and thus was easy to eradicate.

Brent to Kingsbridge – the Primrose Line

The history of the Devon branch lines must by now be rather familiar! Alas, the Kingsbridge line was no different, having been proposed and obtaining its first Act in 1864. Just 4 miles of earthworks had been completed when the money ran out and all work stopped. Nearly twenty years went by before a new company, grandly named The Kingsbridge & Salcombe Railway Company Ltd, was formed in 1882. A year later the company was absorbed by the GWR and following yet more delays the line finally reached Kingsbridge in 1893. This was the same year that the main line had been rebuilt to standard gauge double track. The late completion at least meant that the new line was built in standard gauge.

The main line at South Brent skirts the southern slopes of Dartmoor and its elevation is fairly high at 440 ft – fortunately the river Avon flows down from Dartmoor, around Brent and

Avonwick station with the climb up to the main line starting in the distance. (Lens of Sutton Association)

Gara Bridge, the main station on the route to Kingsbridge though serving a very small community. Most has disappeared today with the station now converted to a private dwelling. (Lens of Sutton Association)

Loddiswell station in 1921 with a stationary goods train. From here the line climbed to Sorley tunnel. (Lens of Sutton Association)

southwards towards the coast, cutting a steadily dropping valley as it goes. The Kingsbridge line takes advantage of this, leaving Brent station and heading south-east for 1½ miles to join the river valley near Avonwick. This section involves sections of 1 in 50 and 1 in 60 before the valley evens the gradients out through Gara Bridge and into Loddiswell. This section follows the beautiful deep wooded river valley, lined in spring with primroses, hence the nickname. At this point, the river very unhelpfully veers westward, leaving the line no choice but to climb over Sorley Hill to reach its destination. The last three miles thus consist of 1½ miles climbing at 1 in 50 and 1 in 76, a 625 yd long tunnel, and a further 1½ miles falling at 1 in 50 and 1 in 60 to reach Kingsbridge. This steep descent to the terminus required goods trains to stop at the summit and pin down the brakes before setting off. The line to Salcombe was never built but horse-drawn coaches and later buses provided a connecting service from Kingsbridge, as did two GWR-owned boats, which ran from 1927 to 1929. A railway booking office remained operational in Salcombe until 1961. All three intermediate stations had camping coaches that relied on paraffin for lighting, cooking and heating in the 1930s. In later years calor gas took over these duties and the coaches lasted until 1962.

Gara Bridge was the main station for trains to pass each other and it was equipped with a good-sized signal box, with 24 levers and a gate wheel to operate one of the two level crossings on the line. Kingsbridge featured the usual array of sidings and a substantial goods shed. The 30-lever signal box hardly changed at all over its life whilst around it there were several modifications to the track layout and sidings. A small engine shed along with a pit and coaling stage completed the scene, but there was never any means to turn locomotives on the line.

The passenger service was remarkably stable, consisting of six trains from Brent and five trains from Kingsbridge. The peak being summer Saturdays in the British Railways era when ten or eleven trains ran, including through trains to Totnes or Newton Abbot, plus through coaches to and from London.

Early locomotives included the hard working 517 class 0-4-2 tanks, usually with four or five four-wheeled coaches. A steam

Kingsbridge terminus, with the little engine shed, pit and water tank. The goods facilities were much more extensive with five sidings, cattle pens and a large goods shed. (Kidderminster Railway Museum)

Today the site is an industrial estate but the station building and the goods shed, shown here, are still standing and in use. (Author)

railmotor was employed in the first twenty or so years of the 20th century but the mainstay of the line were 2-6-2 tank engines of various classes, aided on occasions by pannier tanks. Both goods only and mixed trains ran with the normal rural loads of coal, livestock and general goods though movement of livestock seems to have virtually stopped after 1945. Crabs and lobsters destined for London and Southampton (for the liners), plus rabbits for the Midlands, provided a useful extra income. By 1961 DMUs took over the passenger services, though usually a single car was sufficient; goods traffic was still sometimes steam-hauled, sometimes diesel until 1963 when the line closed. Both Avonwick and Gara Bridge stations are now private dwellings, with virtually all signs of platforms and sidings gone. Kingsbridge station site is a small industrial estate though the goods shed is still clearly standing.

5
The Other Route to Plymouth

Exeter, Yeoford, Okehampton and Plymouth
Callington branch

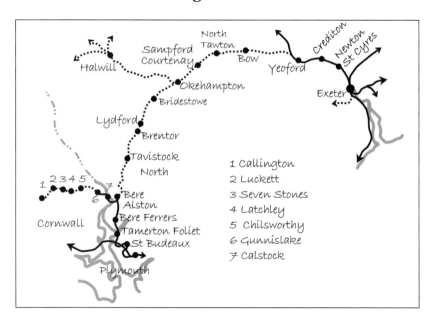

Exeter, Yeoford, Okehampton and Plymouth

The London & South Western Railway's route from Exeter to Barnstaple had been opened in 1855 and, in 1862, the Okehampton Railway was incorporated to construct a line from

Okehampton in 1964 with a stopping train for Padstow and Bude behind a BR class 4 in the bay. A Hymek diesel-hauled train is going on to Plymouth. (Kidderminster Railway Museum)

The same scene today. The station has been lovingly restored with an authentic Southern Railway atmosphere. (Author)

a junction on the Barnstaple line near Coleford, west of Crediton, to Okehampton. The following year, these powers were extended to allow the line to continue to Lydford next to the broad gauge GWR Launceston line from Plymouth. This was to be converted to dual gauge to allow the standard gauge LSWR trains from the Okehampton line to reach Plymouth.

The LSWR had signed an agreement with the GWR and the South Devon Railway not to go beyond Okehampton and so they had to play down their interest in the Okehampton Railway's progress.

In 1865 the Okehampton company changed its name to the

somewhat ambitious Devon & Cornwall Railway, adding further powers to reach Bude and Torrington. The Launceston, Bodmin & Wadebridge Railway Company changed its name at the same time to become the Cornwall Central Railway, adding powers to reach Truro. All this promised a connection for the LSWR to reach its outpost – the Bodmin & Wadebridge Railway, which it had purchased, some say completely illegally, many years before. That the LSWR was behind all of this was hardly secret and so it attempted to get out of its agreement with the GWR but discussions failed and following more skulduggery it eventually won when Parliament came down in favour of open competition rather than the protectionist habits of the South Devon and GWR companies.

Having got as far as Okehampton in 1871, the Devon & Cornwall was absorbed by the LSWR in 1872 and two years later Lydford was finally reached. The link to the dual gauge GWR line was used from 1876, which allowed LSWR trains to continue into Plymouth, and by passing over the GWR main line, through North Road station and then onto its own tracks, it reached its own Devonport station.

The line was not easy with plenty of gradients in the 1 in 80 region, and just beyond Meldon Quarry the spectacular Meldon Viaduct. The line was soon doubled, including the viaduct, which became two virtually identical structures bolted together.

Sharing the little line from Lydford to Plymouth with the GWR was always difficult and the GWR made scant effort to ease the congestion. In 1883 the Plymouth, Devonport & South Western Junction Railway Company was formed to build an independent line from Lydford to Plymouth, which was opened in 1890. It was built with double, standard gauge track throughout and considerable engineering works including three tunnels and many bridges. Though part owned by the LSWR, which indeed operated it from the start, the company had also built and run the Callington branch from Bere Alston. This was an enlargement of the earlier 3 ft 6 in East Cornwall Mineral Railway and opened under a Light Railway Act in 1908. It was finally absorbed by the LSWR in 1922, just in time to become part of the Southern Railway.

Lydford had a GWR side (above right) and a SR side. After 1916 this odd double sided signal box with two lever frames back to back was installed to control all the lines. (Kidderminster Railway Museum)

Brentor SR station. The GWR line passed by, without a station, behind the bushes on the left. (J. H. Aston)

Tavistock (North) looking north. Always a busy station with local trains to and from Plymouth as well as through trains to Exeter and London. The footbridge is now awaiting reuse on the Plym Valley Railway (Author's Collection)

The downside building now in private hands, has hardly changed from the 1950s. The trackbed over the viaduct and to the south is now a footpath. The rest of the station is covered in modern housing. (Author)

Having descended from the hills around Tavistock and into the Tamar valley, the line swept under Brunel's great Saltash Bridge and climbed to reach the GWR line near St Budeaux before burrowing under the GWR line and tunnelling into the Devonport station. Having arrived from the west the LSWR trains usually carried on to the greatly enlarged Plymouth North Road station. Just a year later the LSWR completed its own terminus at Friary on the eastern side of Plymouth to which its main line trains ran.

The passenger service beyond Okehampton was never very intense, with between four and seven trains a day, plus up to

Bere Alston in 1962 with a Callington line train in the bay behind the far waiting room. (Kidderminster Railway Museum)

Devonport station in 1958, the original terminus for the LSWR services. Before the war the whole station was covered in but had these conventional platform canopies built after bomb damage. (Stations UK)

St Budeaux SR station served suburban Plymouth and had to compete with the local tram service. The building was altered several times and by 1980 only the far platform was in use with just a single shelter. (R. K. Blencowe)

seven express trains heading for Plymouth. Sunday services consisted of four local trains, plus just two expresses. Ironically, the best services were in the twenty years following nationalisation in 1948. For many years Okehampton had handled military personnel, horses and equipment heading for the training areas on Dartmoor. The sidings built for this use ended their days accommodating the short-lived car-carrying service that operated from Surbiton, south of London, in the summers of 1960 to 1964.

Okehampton is strictly speaking not 'lost'; the station has been restored and a service operates a short ride to Meldon Quarry. The track (now owned by English China Clay Quarries Ltd) is still down back to Coleford junction and in summer a special DMU service from Exeter operates in conjunction with the Dartmoor Railway.

The LSWR introduced suburban services along its lines in Plymouth, something the GWR had never contemplated but, seeing its rival's success, it quickly followed suit. By 1907 there were some 250 local trains passing through North Road station every weekday, many provided by steam railcars. These consisted of a coach with a small steam engine built in at one

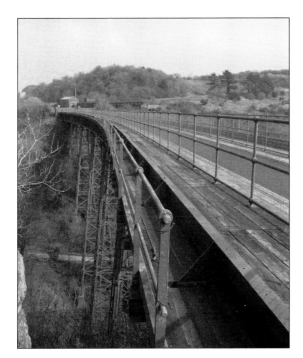

The spectacular Meldon Viaduct, now a pathway and cycle track, which follows the old main line down to Lydford. (Author)

end, driving the bogie wheels at that end – the steam equivalent of the single diesel railcar introduced in the 1930s. These had a vertical boiler and were terrible to drive, with insufficient room and oppressive heat.

The period up to 1914 saw an enormous expansion of Plymouth and the surrounding area; though initiated by the rail services it soon became sustained by an ever-improving system of buses and trams. A link was built between the two lines at St Budeaux during the war and in 1964 this became the normal route for Southern Region trains to reach North Road. The Devonport tunnel and station were then closed. A similar wartime link at Launceston was used in the same way from 1952, with Western Region trains using the Southern, ex-LSWR, station.

Following nationalisation the line became part of the Western

Region in 1963, which must have taken some joy in closing it down in 1968. The line from Meldon Quarry, though, was still producing some 300,000 tons of granite, which saved the eastern section of the route. The passenger service to Okehampton, just short of the quarry, stopped in 1972 but quarry traffic still uses the line today. There is now an excellent cycle path alongside the line from Okehampton to Meldon Quarry, which then follows the redundant track bed to just outside Lydford. This includes crossing the Meldon Viaduct so beware if you have a fear of heights.

Callington branch

This branch started life as the east Cornwall Mineral Railway, a 3 ft 6 in gauge line that brought minerals from the Callington area to a quay on the river Tamar at Calstock. Opened in 1872, it served granite quarries plus mines extracting copper, tin, silver and arsenic. The Plymouth, Devonport & South Western Junction Railway had included in its Act the purchasing and

The bridge over the river Tamar where our line leaves Devon. The old 3 ft 6 in line came down to the quay on the river's edge via an incline. The short-lived wagon lift is under construction in this 1904 photo but was removed in 1934. (Kidderminster Railway Museum)

Gunnislake station in 1962, two years before steam finished on the line. (Stations UK)

conversion to conventional gauge of the mineral line. Undertaken under the Light Railway Acts, the section from the main line at Bere Alston to Calstock was built during the 1904–1908 period and included the Calstock Viaduct over the Tamar. The engineer for the new line was the redoubtable Colonel Stephens, though the viaduct itself was constructed by Galbraith & Church. Colonel Stephens took many small rural lines under his management and, by applying an austere regime, he kept many running well into the 1920s and 30s, way beyond their true commercial life expectancy. Taken into the Southern Railway in 1923, the line operated a steady service of around six trains until DMUs took over in 1964, after which eight trains ran on weekdays

In 1966 the section beyond Gunnislake was closed and a DMU service still runs from Plymouth. This uses the now singled LSWR line to Bere Alston, where it reverses onto the Callington branch as far as Gunnislake. A trial to use Pacer diesel units on this service in 1986 failed as the many tight curves on the line beyond Bere Alston wore the wheels down at an alarming rate. The Pacer units were very much like a single-decker bus with two fixed axles. It was because these axles, unlike a bogie, couldn't turn to follow a tight curve that the problems arose.

6
Halwill, the Unknown Junction

Okehampton to Bude
Halwill to Launceston
Halwill to Torrington

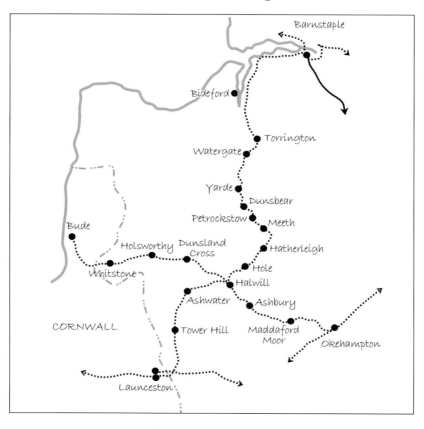

Okehampton to Bude

With hindsight we can see that bells should have rung when a
line struggled to get enthusiastic backing but, in the 1880s, the car
and lorry were still science fiction in rural Devon. The Bude line
was typical of many such lines, its original Act having long
lapsed when a line was constructed in 1879, from a junction on
the Devon and Cornwall line just west of the Meldon Viaduct to
Holsworthy. On its route it passed the small hamlet at Halwill,
which was to know so much activity in the coming years. A local
company had obtained powers to extend to Bude but that failed
to happen. Eventually in 1898 the LSWR extended the line,
building a nine-arch concrete viaduct to leave Holsworthy, this
being the first time pre-cast concrete blocks had been used on
such a large structure. The terminus in Bude had been positioned
on the outskirts of the town to placate the residents of nearby
Stratton (Bude was much smaller than Stratton in 1898) and a
branch extended down to the canal basin. The Bude Canal, along
with its basin and sea lock, had been built to move the limy sea

*Ashbury station in 1964 with a BR 4 class 2-6-2 loco in charge of an
Okehampton to Bude train. (J. H. Aston)*

85

An ex-Bude goods train hauled by an 'N' class loco, approaches Halwill Junction in 1964 whilst the single coach train for Torrington waits in its own bay platform. (Kidderminster Railway Museum)

Holsworthy in 1964 with trains to and from Bude passing. This was the most important stop on the line with a turntable, goods shed, abattoir and timber yard. Today it all lies beneath a supermarket though both viaducts are still standing. (J. H. Aston)

86

Whitstone and Bridgerule station was, alas, miles from both villages. Here in 1954 two coaches and a van head for Bude. On the right are goods wagons probably all carrying agricultural products. (Stations UK)

The station today is in private hands with the space between the platforms filled in. (Author)

sand inland for use as a fertiliser but now the railway could bring in better 'modern' fertilisers and the use of sand quickly faded. Ironically the sea lock and canal are still active and working, whilst the railway has long since disappeared.

The service on the line was, unhappily, always slow and poor – a classic case of too little, too late. Most trains consisted of coaches from Exeter and further afield, which would split at Halwill into sections for Padstow and Bude, two coaches making up the usual Bude train. There was also an Okehampton to Bude service, which connected with Exeter to Plymouth trains. Summer holiday traffic was another thing altogether. In

Bude station in 1932, with a rake of coaches parked on the run round loop. (Brunel University/ Mowat Collection)

The only remaining feature left in Bude is the bridge that took the harbour branch over the river. Now part of a pathway. (Author)

the 1930s the platform at Bude was extended to take ten-coach trains. The line carried a fair amount of freight – the inevitable coal plus cattle and carcasses and hides from the slaughterhouses at Halwill, Holsworthy and Bude. Just how much meat travelled by rail can be gauged from the fact that the Halwill slaughterhouse alone dealt with over 45,000 animals a year in the 1930s. Its products would leave Halwill at 5 pm and be in London or the Midlands before dawn the next morning. Until myxomatosis decimated them, large quantities of dead rabbits were sent from Bude, as indeed they were from many West Country stations.

Early locomotives included class O2 and M7 tank engines, the N class workhorses and the elegant T9 'Greyhounds'. The Bulleid Pacifics rarely ran to Bude as the turntable was too small to carry them. In the last few years class 3, 2-6-2 and class 4, 2-6-4 tank engines gave way to DMUs, often a single car. Alas, it all closed in 1966. Holsworthy station is now a supermarket and Bude station has vanished beneath a housing estate.

Halwill to Launceston

Despite the early hopes, the Cornwall Central Railway (see Chapter 5) had in fact built nothing and it took a new Act in 1882 to get things moving. The line was to leave the Bude branch at Halwill, whose station now became a junction, and head through very spartan lands towards Launceston, which was reached in 1886. Though we are now in Cornwall the enthusiasm, or rather lack of it, for this line can be gauged from

Halwill Junction in 1926 with a train signalled for the Launceston line headed by a class 460 engine. (Kidderminster Railway Museum)

89

The only trace left in Halwill today, the Junction Inn which apart from the addition of the front porch is just as it was in the early 1970s when the author stayed there. (Author)

the fact that it took another nine years to complete the 30 miles to Wadebridge. Launceston was pleased to at last have a direct route to Exeter but, as so often happened once cars and buses arrived, the enthusiasm vanished.

The line was never really busy but traffic in meat and cattle added to the meagre passenger figures. Events livened up on summer Saturdays when holiday traffic burst upon the scene, with London connections to both Bude and Padstow fighting for access to the single track lines. Halwill became renowned for these sporadic bursts of frantic activity before slipping back to steady but infrequent local traffic.

Through coaches from London stopped in 1964, as did the freight trains. Diesels appeared a year later but it was all in vain; these lines part of the sadly nicknamed 'Withered Arm', were

The SR station in Launceston in 1959 with a two-coach train heading for Okehampton. (Kidderminster Railway Museum)

The site today completely bereft of railway features except for the narrow gauge line laid on the old trackbed heading west beyond the bridge. (Author)

never going to survive and all closed in 1966. Halwill station is now under housing, approached by the appropriately-named 'Beeching Close'.

Halwill to Torrington

In 1880 a 3 ft gauge mineral line had been constructed by the North Devon Clay Company from Torrington to its clay works near Marland. In 1914 the North Devon & Cornwall Junction Light Railway obtained an order to construct a standard gauge

91

Torrington station with a steam train ready to leave for Barnstaple and a DMU waiting to venture down to Halwill. (E. T. Gill)

Today the station houses a café, a cycle hire company and a few railway relics plus the delightful Tarka Trail, a walking route and cycle way along the former line. (Author)

Petrockstow station today, once in the heart of the china clay area, is in the middle of the Tarka Trail. (Author)

Meeth station, which was also kept busy with china clay traffic, is now the southern starting point of the Tarka Trail. (Author)

93

Hatherleigh station in the late 1950s, with the usual single car DMU setting off for Torrington. As always the station is clean and bright. (E. T. Gill)

line between Torrington and Halwill, using most of the older 3 ft gauge trackbed. Construction was delayed by the First World War until 1922 when work started under the renowned Colonel Stephens (see Chapter 5). After leaving Torrington station the line immediately crosses the river, originally on a fine timber viaduct but this was not strong enough to carry even the needs of a 'light' railway and it was rebuilt with conventional steel girders resting on masonry columns. In 1925 the new line was fully open and was operated by the Southern Railway, successors to the LSWR, even though the original company remained independent (in theory) until nationalisation in 1948. Until 1925 Bideford had been regarded as the end of the line from Exeter, with the Ilfracombe route regarded as a branch but the Southern decided to exchange these two 'ends' and the Bideford, Torrington and Halwill traffic now became the branch and Ilfracombe the main line.

The passenger service beyond Torrington was always infrequent and usually just one coach was sufficient, though many of the trains were mixed passenger and goods. The largest town near the line was Hatherleigh, which, in traditional rural fashion, had its station nearly two miles away. Following an attack on the local police by the gangs building the line in 1923, Hatherleigh turned its back on the railway, leaving china clay as the only real traffic. On a few occasions when snow closed the main line around Okehampton the line saw the passage of the Atlantic Coast Express (see Chapter 7) heading to and from Wadebridge and Padstow – not, however, pulled by a main line Pacific locomotive!

Passenger services ceased in 1965 and the line to the Meeth china clay works was then run as a long siding all the way to Barnstaple. In 1982 even the clay traffic had moved to road transport and the line closed completely. These days the Tarka Trail, mentioned in the next chapter, uses the trackbed from Meeth and provides a very enjoyable walk. At present the trackbed between Meeth and Petrockstow is used by a private company and the Tarka Trail runs alongside.

The Tarka Trail showing the excellent pathway and the occasional artwork along the way. (Author)

7
Barnstaple, Capital of the North

Barnstaple to Torrington
Barnstaple to Ilfracombe
The Lynton & Barnstaple Railway
Bideford, Westward Ho! and Appledore

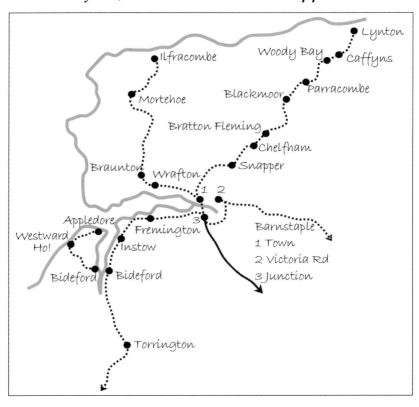

Barnstaple to Torrington

Prior to the 1840s, most coastal trading ships were unable to reach Barnstaple and instead docked at Appledore, where their loads were transferred to barges, which could navigate the shallow waters of the river Taw. To improve on this somewhat convoluted system, the Taw Vale Railway & Dock Company built a dock at Fremington and a standard gauge horse-drawn railway from the quay into Barnstaple, which opened in 1848. In 1854, soon after they had extended to Crediton using the broad gauge, the old horse-drawn section was rebuilt as a broad gauge line and in 1855 extended along the edge of the river Torridge to reach Bideford. This side of the river is known as East-the-Water as Bideford itself is on the western bank. The route so far had been virtually flat and easy to build. The LSWR owned shares in the Taw Vale Railway and eventually, in 1862, it leased the Taw Vale Railway, plus the line from Crediton to Exeter originally

Barnstaple Junction today, devoid of virtually every facility. The platform on the right had lines on both sides giving three working platforms. The goods yard and loco facilities are all now under a retail park. (Author)

Bideford station in 1939 with the Royal Hotel entrance just behind the camera. The road under bridge was raised to platform level after the line closed and makes a peculiar break in the station today. (Stations UK)

built by the independent Exeter and Crediton Railway Company. The following year it added a third rail to enable its standard gauge trains to reach Barnstaple and Bideford from Exeter.

Various schemes were proposed to take the line further south, in particular to reach Torrington, a town of not inconsiderable size. Extensions on to Okehampton also featured in this period of hopeful proposals. Eventually in 1872 the line was extended to Torrington, or at least to a site in the river valley some three-quarters of a mile from, and 200 feet below, Torrington itself. This was built to standard gauge by the LSWR using much of the old Rolle Canal. Bideford station was moved southwards, opposite the road bridge from the town, as part of the extension work and the old broad gauge station became an enlarged goods yard.

China clay came to Torrington via a 3 ft mineral line, which had a single interchange siding at the back of the goods sidings.

This mineral line was later re-laid in standard gauge as an end-on extension of the line from Bideford and was extended beyond the china clay areas to reach Halwill Junction.

The original service to Torrington consisted of five return trips on weekdays plus a single early trip on Sundays but this soon increased until a peak around in the 1930s of fourteen weekday trains and seven on Sundays, and the Atlantic Coast Express (see next section) had coaches for both Bideford and Torrington. The goods traffic proved very important, with milk from Torrington destined for London figuring significantly; this peaked in 1957 at 2 million gallons. Fremington Quay, modernised by the Southern Railway in the 1930s, became the second busiest port

Instow station in 1939 showing both platforms in use and the small engine shed which later became a private siding. (Stations UK)

Instow station today, with the Tarka Trail running along the old trackbed. The signal box is restored though the other platform has been filled in. (Author)

99

Torrington station with a three-coach train from Barnstaple behind an LMS class 2 in 1964 (Kidderminster Railway Museum)

Today the station still has a railway theme, but it is now used as a café and residence. (Author)

in Devon after Plymouth, carrying up to 30,000 tons of china clay a year until its eventual closure in 1970.

In the 1950s a new power station was constructed at East Yelland and extensive sidings from the Bideford–Torrington line were put in place for construction traffic. Coal came by sea and only very rarely was any brought to the power station by rail. Generation of electricity started in 1953 and ended 31 years later in 1984.

Following reorganisation of the West of England lines in 1958, the route came under the Western Region but ever-declining use saw the end of passenger services to Torrington in 1965. Milk traffic lasted until 1978 and the china clay traffic ceased in 1980, with the line closing completely in 1982. Today the entire line is part of the Tarka Trail and can be walked or cycled. Both Bideford and Instow stations have been partly restored, along with their signal boxes and track in an attempt to recall those years when they were served by rail from far off cities.

Barnstaple to Ilfracombe

Ilfracombe was a long established seaside resort from the earliest Victorian times. Proposals to reach it by rail had been made several times, two as early as the 1840s. In 1863 the LSWR had acquired the whole Exeter to Barnstaple route and the link to Ilfracombe was again discussed. Two routes had been proposed. One, to the east, was very expensive, while the other had the usual landowner problems.

Sir William Williams owned a near derelict property, Heanton Court, the grounds of which ran down to the Taw estuary, and he didn't want the railway to run across his views. He had actively backed some of the east route schemes, which would have used a route through Bittadon, completely avoiding his land and also the village of Braunton. All manner of alternatives were proposed including even tunnelling under the river. Eventually Sir William Williams withdrew his objections and in 1870 the Barnstaple & Ilfracombe Company (in reality a subsidiary of the LSWR) was able to proceed.

Though Sir William is often cited as the cause of the delays there was also considerable apathy both in Ilfracombe and Barnstaple. At the first meeting of the company it was reported: 'It is a matter of notoriety that the amount of subscriptions forthcoming from the district is so exceedingly small that it would be useless to attempt the construction of the line unless some substantial subsidy can be obtained from the LSWR.'

The line was to be built under a Light Railway Order though it was upgraded to a normal status in 1887. The construction was slow and difficult, there was a shortage of labour and the route posed many difficult sections – but despite this the line was completed in 1874.

Barnstaple Junction in 1955 with the Ilfracombe lines going off to the left and the Bideford lines passing under the photographer. The footbridge has long gone, as indeed has the bridge from which this shot was taken. (Kidderminster Railway Museum)

It has been suggested that the long and protracted battle to reach Ilfracombe from Exeter – it had been 30 years – had damaged the public's image of the North Devon resorts but in 1874 there was no faster way to reach this dramatic coastline. The delay did, however, suggest a deep local disinterest in the scheme, which like so many rural lines was, in reality, only just viable.

During the late 1880s the line was doubled except for the Barnstaple Junction to Pottington (just west of the town) section, which would have been prohibitively expensive. Amusingly, the trackbed had been purchased with enough room for double track but the single line had been built in the centre, thus causing extra expense in laying the second track as the original track had to be moved over first.

The line formed an end-on junction with the Exeter lines in Barnstaple Junction station from where it swung sharply north and east to cross the river Taw to the new Barnstaple Quay

102

The bridge over the Taw which limited the weight and width of everything that went up the Ilfracombe line. Seen here with a train approaching the Junction station in 1964 pulled by a North British type 2 diesel hydraulic locomotive D6316. (Kidderminster Railway Museum)

Barnstaple Town station awaiting its fate in the early 1970s. The right-hand side of the platform served the Lynton narrow gauge line. (Author)

103

station. Just before crossing the river there was a siding into the Raleigh Cabinet Works, built in 1890, plus a line into a small riverside wharf. The bridge over the Taw was a terrifyingly fragile affair that stood on equally thin wrought iron piles sunk into the riverbed and filled with concrete. It was this structure that imposed both width and weight limitation on the engines. Like all the original stations along the line, Quay station was a single platform with a single track and indeed, except for the later addition of a passing loop, this station remained this way to the end. In 1886 the name was changed to Barnstaple Town and in 1898 it was rebuilt to accommodate the Lynton & Barnstaple line, which terminated here. From here the line crossed over the Yeo on a small swing bridge provided to let ships of up to 250 tons reach the wharves beside the river. In 1891 a ship became grounded whilst passing through the swing bridge thus closing the route. Fortunately there was a train on the Ilfracombe side, which operated from Ilfracombe to just before the bridge where passengers were led by road to the Town station to continue their journey.

The line set off west and then north across relatively flat land to Braunton, a village that later was to have a RAF airfield (Chivenor) to swell its commerce though the airfield never had a halt or even a siding for fuel. North of Braunton a dramatic change took place as the line started a 6-mile climb, much of it at 1 in 40, to reach Mortehoe some 600 ft above sea level. The severity of this climb needed extra banking locomotives for longer or heavier trains and these were kept in a siding south of Braunton station, ready to be coupled onto the rear of trains before they tackled the ascent. Mortehoe station was – following the tradition in rural Devon of siting stations at a puzzling distance from the community they served – two miles from the village of the same name and also two miles from the considerably larger Woolacombe, which was added, somewhat belatedly, to the station name in 1950. Banking was also needed for the long summer holiday trains climbing out of Ilfracombe and, on busy days, extended trains of holidaymakers would pass at Mortehoe station, both with banking engines panting from their exertions, all four engines making a fine sight.

The doyen of the West Country class locos 34001 'Exeter' coasts down the line towards Ilfracombe in 1952. (Kidderminster Railway Museum)

Halfway down the 1 in 36 descent the line pierced an outcrop in two short single tunnels. One is still open as part of the footpath from Mortehoe to Ilfracombe. (Author)

From here the line descended to Ilfracombe down a hair-raising gradient of 1 in 36 terminating on a long, wide embankment that held the station, goods yards and storage sidings. Yet again the station was still two thirds of a mile from the town centre. In the late 1800s this didn't matter too much as visitors came from far away and finishing the journey by horse-drawn coach or cart was looked on as only a minor annoyance, just as taking a taxi might be today. The station had a single platform but there were lines on both sides allowing two trains to be serviced at the same time. There were several long carriage sidings, an engine shed, which was enlarged and moved in the 1920s, along with a good-sized turntable. The original engine shed was wooden and in 1910 suffered the indignity of having the rear wall demolished by an over enthusiastic locomotive. As often happens the station was altered several times with the platform extended and raised, extra sidings built and changes to the platform canopy and a new signal box. A goods shed plus an abattoir completed the facilities. As mentioned, the town was still a good distance away – not just horizontally but also vertically, being some 200 ft lower, thus requiring some stout performances from the horses drawing the carts and coaches.

The train service peaked in the early 1900s with the summer season boasting seventeen trains each way on weekdays; the Sunday service, however, was always poor or non-existent. The Southern Railway developed an interesting service from London, mainly for the holiday traffic, where the train left the capital with upwards of 14 coaches. It then started a process of breaking up into sets of coaches each destined for a different seaside town. The most famous of these trains was the Atlantic Coast Express, a most apt name suggested by a guard from Waterloo station. Started in 1926 this train had coaches for Exeter, Sidmouth, Exmouth, Plymouth, Ilfracombe (usually the largest section), Bideford, Torrington, Bude and Padstow. A short-lived but glorious all Pullman car service known as the Devon Belle ran to Plymouth and Ilfracombe from 1947 until 1954. This train included an observation car, which was turned on the Ilfracombe turntable so as to be able to take its position as the last coach on the return journey. Even the GWR had a four-coach set on the Cornish Riviera Express, including a restaurant coach, which was slipped at Taunton and brought to Ilfracombe via the Taunton to Barnstaple line.

These through trains achieved a journey time from London of just over 5 hours and just over 5½ hours for the GWR route. Through trains from Bradford and Liverpool ran on summer Saturdays but took over 10 hours for the trip. These racy journeys changed their pace after Exeter with a journey time of nearly an hour for the 15 miles from Barnstaple to Ilfracombe (which slowly improved to around 45 minutes in the 20th century). This sounds incredibly slow to us today but there were two reasons. Firstly, the line had several speed limits – Barnstaple Junction to Braunton was limited to 55 mph (after 1969 reduced to 15 mph over the Taw bridge and 40 mph to Braunton), the climb to Mortehoe was set at 40 mph and the descent to Ilfracombe was limited to 30 mph. The second limitation, which we forget today, was the time taken to get passengers and their luggage off the train. The intermediate stations all had holiday customers and a

Ilfracombe station was built on a embankment that jutted out high over the town. The long single platform was covered at the buffer end where a DMU waits to return to Barnstable in 1969. (Stations UK)

107

family with suitcases and prams took a long time to get sorted out. It was not unknown for a long train of holidaymakers to take a full hour to clear at Ilfracombe station. There is an amusing story of a guard on a departing train who in order to see his driver had to claw his way through the thronging masses. He duly waved his flag but was unable to get back to his train as it drew out of the platform. He rejoined his train at Mortehoe following a very hasty taxi ride!

Goods traffic remained fairly steady over many years, usually consisting of two trains to Ilfracombe and back each day. The first left at 5.10 am (after 1938 at 6.54 am), taking the mail and papers plus goods, the second around 10 am, carrying mixed goods. Return workings were in the afternoon.

Problems were relatively few, though in severe winters the Mortehoe area had very heavy snowfalls, which closed the line on three occasions.

Being built as a light railway the locomotives originally posed a problem; they had to be powerful to work the steep gradients but they had to be lightweight, not an easy mix to achieve. In 1870 Joseph Beattie had designed a 0-6-0 engine but he wasn't happy with it and so asked the locomotive builders Beyer Peacock for advice and they suggested a 4-4-0 but William Beattie, who now succeeded his father as Locomotive Engineer of the LSWR, didn't like this idea. Eventually in 1872 Beyer Peacock supplied their standard light 0-6-0 engines, which had been designed for overseas companies faced with hard gradients, in particular in Sweden. These became known as the 'Ilfracombe Goods' and though a fraction heavier than the Light Railway Act allowed they did sterling work; eventually eight were built.

In the 1890s the locomotive engineer William Adams' T1 0-4-4 and Jubilee 0-4-2s were based at Barnstaple and were used on the Ilfracombe services, the track having been brought up to normal standards by this time. In the 1900s Dugald Drummond's excellent M7 0-4-4 tank engines appeared and in the 1920s the versatile N class 2-6-0 joined the M7s to form the mainstay of the services right through to the end of steam in 1964. Throughout this period GWR trains from the Taunton–Barnstaple line worked through to Ilfracombe, usually hauled by 4300 or 6300 class 2-6-0 locomotives, which incidentally had to have their steps cut back to give a width of 8 ft 4 in – that bridge in Barnstaple again. In 1941 Bullied's powerful West Country Pacifics arrived, hauling the main line through services and were found working on the Ilfracombe branch right through to the end. The rebuilt versions of these engines were too heavy for the Barnstaple bridge and only the original air-smoothed casing versions remained working this part of Devon. These locomotives were too long to be turned on the Barnstaple turntable and often ran 'light' to Ilfracombe just to be turned around. In the 1950s the occasional Ivatt 2-6-2 tank engine would be used along with BR standard 4MT class 2-6-4.

In 1964 steam ended, the Ilfracombe turntable was removed and DMUs and diesel locomotives took over. As was common for a line no longer regarded as important, these locomotives were older units displaced from main line duties – Western Region 'Warships' plus the occasional Hymek or Type 2. In 1967 the line was singled and, surprisingly, the track was renewed in 1969 just six months before the inevitable end, which came in 1970. Holiday passengers for Ilfracombe fell from a useful 5,000-plus on a summer Saturday in 1957, to just 460 by 1967. There followed a gallant attempt to save the line as a preserved steam railway but this failed and the track was lifted in 1975. The Taw bridge in Barnstaple was removed three years later.

Today the trackbed from the old Barnstaple Town station towards Braunton is a part of the South West Coastal Path and the descent from Mortehoe towards Ilfracombe is walkable.

The Lynton & Barnstaple Railway

The Lynton & Barnstaple Railway can only be described as a gem; that it didn't manage to survive into the era of the preservation movement is seen by many as a tragedy.

So what made this line so endearing? Firstly, it was a narrow gauge line, the track spaced at just 1 ft 11½ in, but despite its diminutive gauge this was a real railway constructed to very high standards and not a mineral line with ambition to one day carry passengers. It was also a tourist line built to exploit the excursion traffic to Lynton and Lynmouth. In the event it carried goods as well but as mentioned in the introduction, the core tourist business was destined to wilt when faced with the car.

The company chairman was Sir George Newnes, the publisher, who lived in Lynton and who had observed the horse-drawn charabancs coming from Ilfracombe and Barnstaple loaded with visitors. Some 30,000 arrived this way each summer and Sir George believed that a railway line could thrive on this traffic. A quick glance at any map will show that we are talking of crossing the edge of Exmoor, hardly the ideal terrain for either horse buses or railways – thus the choice of a narrow gauge line, which could twist and turn along the narrow valleys. Incorporated in 1895 construction began promptly but the contractor, a James Nuttall of Manchester, had accepted the company's somewhat over-optimistic cost estimates. Following an acrimonious court case and appeal, Mr Nuttall promptly departed from Devon leaving the company to complete the line itself, which with all credit it did, with the line opening in 1898.

The engines were supplied by the Manning Wardle Company who delivered three charming 2-6-2 tank engines in 1897 – these

Barnstaple Town station around 1930 with the Lynton train ready to depart. Even today one can just make out where the buffers were though the route through to Pilton yard is completely gone. (Lens of Sutton Association)

110

were named *Yeo, Exe* and *Taw*. By the opening year the board feared that they would need a fourth engine and because of the rush, an American 2-4-2 engine was purchased from the Baldwin Locomotive Company of Philadelphia. Shipped in parts it was assembled in the railway's workshops in Pilton (just north-west of Barnstaple Quay) and named *Lyn*. Sixteen coaches had been ordered from the Bristol Carriage and Wagon works, fitted with roller bearing, a novel feature that unfortunately didn't last too well and they were later changed to plain bearings. Goods wagons were also ordered though exactly how many and when is not clear. Sir George was set on the holiday passenger traffic, and goods traffic was not part of the plan. In practice the passengers didn't desert the horse-drawn coaches and the goods traffic saved the company from losing money. Signalling was installed on the 'main' line and any passing loops but not elsewhere. The railway had wanted to terminate adjacent to the LSWR line at Barnstaple Town but the LSWR wasn't particularly interested until the Lynton & Barnstaple threatened to build its own station, after which the LSWR rebuilt its station slightly to the north to provide a platform side for the new line.

With the asset of hindsight one has to wonder if Sir George's judgment was really very sound. Firstly, the terminus in Lynton, originally destined to be in the town, was built instead some one third of a mile away. Some say it was Sir George who didn't want to see a railway from his house, others that Sir George refused to sell the company the necessary land. Personally I have doubts, as a few minutes with an OS map will show that to reach much closer to Lynton would have needed impossibly steep gradients or else massive earthworks. The other doubt concerns the imminent arrival of motor buses, indeed Sir George purchased two Milnes-Daimler vehicles in 1903, just five years after the railway opened, in a last ditch attempt to get at the Ilfracombe bus excursion traffic. It failed and the buses were sold to the GWR who used them in Cornwall. That such a large project as the Lynton & Barnstaple Railway was undertaken when those who followed the transport advances would surely have known of the imminent arrival of motor buses is an interesting thought.

Despite the short summer holiday season the little line made a modest profit and in 1923 became part of the Southern Railway. The Southern took its newly acquired line very seriously, purchasing a forth Manning Wardle engine for £2,450 in 1925; this was named *Lew*. The SR also invested in improvements to the rolling stock, the track and the stations. In what seems an extravagant gesture it purchased two breakdown cranes which, thankfully, were rarely used.

Alas, the slump of the 1929–30 period dealt a fatal blow to the little line, which never recovered. The Southern Railway, unable to see any future, closed the line in 1935. The last train was so busy that two engines (*Yeo* and *Lew*) were needed to pull the nine coaches loaded with some 300 people to Lynton. The line was immediately dismantled with all the rolling stock sold off at bargain prices. The five engines fetched just £236, the youngest, *Lew*, being shipped to Brazil for use on a coffee plantation.

Fortunately the line was well photographed and today a few of the stations survive as private residences. The only major structure, the Chelfham Viaduct, also still stands, now a listed

Chelfham viaduct was the only large engineering work on the line and is a listed structure. Completely cleaned in 2000 it is still eyecatching. (Author)

Chelfham station in 1935, with a posed shot just a few days before closure. (Kidderminster Railway Museum)

structure and refurbished in 2000. Parts of the trackbed can still be found but, despite much talk, there seems little chance of the line being rebuilt. There is, however, a short section near Woody Bay that now runs steam trains and, who knows, it may well expand.

The route left Barnstaple Town station and immediately curved right to follow the river Yeo. The track crossed over two level crossings, now buried beneath two roundabouts, and soon reached the Pilton works, which included an engine shed, carriage sheds and a workshop. Parts of the site still exist as a garage. Quickly passing through the Barnstaple outskirts it regained the river valley, which it followed, mostly clinging to the eastern side. After around 3 miles it reached Snapper halt, which served a very small community. The line now briefly crossed over the river and back before starting to climb more seriously towards the 70 ft high viaduct and Chelfham station. This was the first station, with a passing loop and a small station building. The climb, often around 1 in 50, continued ever higher

Bratton Fleming in 1910 with the station staff and one passenger posing for the camera. (Lens of Sutton Association)

The delightful little train of two coaches and a van making its way along Parracombe bank, en route for Barnstaple, around 1930. (Brunel University/ Mowat Collection)

Woody Bay station, not as one might think in the 1930s but in 2007. Beautifully restored and the home of the Lynton & Barnstaple Railway, which runs trains over 1½ miles of track. (Author)

above the river valley until reaching Bratton Fleming, again with a passing loop, sidings and station buildings.

Just before Bratton station there was a small quarry, which provided ballast for the line. Bratton Fleming and Parracombe were the only sizable villages along the whole route. There is an interesting photo taken during the construction, which shows the valley almost completely devoid of trees, whereas today the forestation is dense. The line now left the river valley and entered a series of tight curves and cuttings before rejoining the river valley and finally running through a large S-shaped curve to reach Blackmoor station. After the line closed this area was flooded to form the Wistlandpound reservoir. Blackmoor station had a passing loop, sidings and a goods shed plus the first of three large Bavarian style station buildings. Today the station is in use as a pub.

The line now manoeuvred around the hills, accompanied today by the A39 road, passing around Parracombe in a long curve, which included Parracombe halt equipped with just a simple shelter. Next, some 16 miles from Barnstaple, was Woody

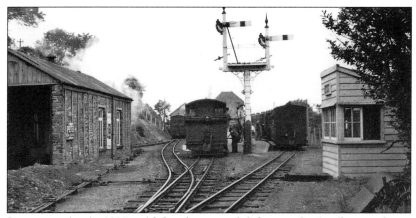

Lynton station in 1935, with barely a month left to go, busier than at almost any time before! (Kidderminster Railway Museum)

Bay station with passing loop, sidings and the second large station building. This was, however, some 2½ miles from the real Woody Bay and, at 980 ft high, in the most sparse section of the whole route. The line now started a steep descent towards Lynton along the edge of the West Lyn river valley and through a small halt at Caffyns, built to serve a nearby golf course. Lynton station, 19 miles from the start was perched 750 ft above sea level and 250 ft above the town it served. It boasted a passing loop, sidings and a goods shed plus a small locomotive shed. The platform had a line on both sides though one side was little more than a bay.

The journey took one and a half hours, due, I suspect, to stopping at every station and the leisurely handling of traffic at the stations; this was, nevertheless, twice as fast as the horse-drawn coach service.

Bideford, Westward Ho! and Appledore

This odd little railway was very short-lived having been built in 1901 and dismantled during the 1914–18 war. The standard gauge line left from Bideford Quay and headed west through the town towards the sea, where it turned north and followed the shoreline to Westward Ho!. Built to capture holiday traffic it was extended in 1908 to Appledore. This rather sad history seems to be of the 'someone built it, it ran and then it closed' variety whereas in fact the little line had all the usual problems we associate with larger enterprises.

Historically both Bideford and Appledore were centres of shipbuilding, indeed Appledore continues to this day. The first scheme for a railway in the area was for a line from the Taw Vale, Bideford line, across the river Torridge to Northam and on to Clovelly, Hartland and Bude. What the cost would have been doesn't bear thinking about! In the 1860s an Act was obtained for the building of a line from near Northam to Appledore, with a branch to Westward Ho! but nothing was done and the Act lapsed in 1870.

Eventually in 1896 the Bideford, Westward Ho! & Appledore Railway Company obtained authorisation for a standard gauge line. Constructed as far as Northam by Charles Shadwell of Blackburn, it cost considerably more than the estimated £50,000 and in the following court action Mr Shadwell was found guilty of 'wilfully deceiving' the company and was fined £7,500. Early in 1900 the railway had become a subsidiary of the vast British Electric Traction Group who promoted tramways both in the UK and overseas. They had ideas of a tramway to Hartland, which would have incorporated the Bideford, Westward Ho! & Appledore line.

The line started on the quayside at Bideford and here it was built as a tramway with the roadway, constructed from wooden blocks, flush to the tops of the rails. There was a small coal siding, which it seems was rarely used. The railway company soon realised it needed a means of running the engine around the train and applied to add a second line to form a loop; however, the council objected. Following the usual controversy the railway built a loop but the council promptly secured an injunction and forced its removal. The company appealed to the Board of Trade and the loop was re-laid in 1903, though as one might expect there was always slight antagonism between the council and the

A train has just arrived at Bideford Quay in 1910. The engine will run round using the much disputed loop, nearer to the camera, before setting off back to Westward Ho! This was the odd engine that was placed on the line facing Bideford. (Kidderminster Railway Museum)

railway. At this time the railway had to man the level crossings. In 1908 an extension to Appledore was built and the entire line was then operated as a light railway, which meant that it only needed to protect the level crossing with cattle guards.

At the end of the quay the line crossed over a reclaimed creek, which had been one of the small shipbuilding yards. The stream had been culverted and this led to claims of flooding due to the restricted waterway to the river Torridge. The route now headed west, past the company's maintenance yards, and through six request halts including a short section of 1 in 47 gradient, before reaching Westward Ho!. The Northam Burrows Hotel and Villa Company had developed this area before the railway came and indeed was associated with the original railway company. Following the publication of Kingsley's *Westward Ho!* in 1855, the area and indeed the hotel company saw a great increase in tourists. Unfortunately there was now a regular bus service from the main line station across the river in Bideford direct to Westward Ho!. So the poor little railway didn't really get its share of the prosperity.

The railway had three new 2-4-2 tank engines, named *Grenville*, *Kingsley* and *Torridge*, built by the Hunslet Engine Co of Leeds, plus six American style, elaborately decorated, teak coaches. As was normal practice for tramways, the locomotives were provided with side plates over the wheels and cowcatchers were later fitted at the front. Strangely two of the locomotives were loaded onto the track facing Westward Ho! and one facing Bideford and, as there was no turntable, they worked that way for the entire life of the railway. There was limited signalling, which was supplied by Saxby & Farmer. Like its more famous neighbour, the Lynton & Barnstaple, everything was built to a high standard. The peak summer timetable featured seventeen journeys over the line starting at 9.30 am – the line never sought the attention of local working folk. Much of the time a single coach sufficed and the traffic, alas, never came. The eleven stations spread over 7 route miles must have been very quiet and lonely despite the good train service. Though it never paid a dividend, it remained individual to the end in 1917 when the government requisitioned the locomotives and all services ended.

On Sunday 29th July, temporary track was laid over the Bideford road bridge to enable the engines to be trundled across the river to near the Royal Hotel. On the following day they ran into the LSWR goods yard and so joined their larger brothers.

Westward Ho! station with two summer service trains crossing. This 1910 view shows the American style of the coaches. (Brunel University/Clinker Collection)

8
South of Exmoor

The Devon & Somerset Railway
Tiverton to Tiverton Junction
The Exe Valley lines
The Hemyock branch – the Culm Valley line

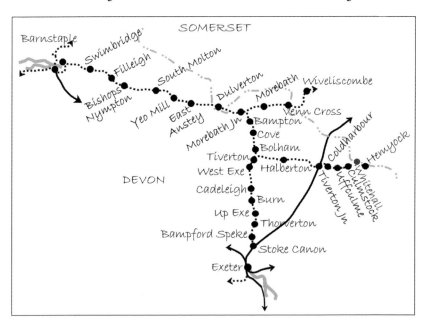

The Devon & Somerset Railway

Much to the annoyance of the LSWR, which had taken over the Exeter to Barnstaple line, the Devon & Somerset Railway Company opted for a broad gauge line linking with the Bristol & Exeter Railway close to Taunton. Following the usual financial

Barnstaple Victoria Road station, the terminus of the GWR line from Taunton, taken in 1956. In the far distance the link to the SR lines left through what is now a Tesco supermarket. (Brunel University/Mowat Collection)

struggles the line was opened in 1873 (it had been authorised in 1864). During construction in 1866 funds fell so low that many of the navvies were discharged. Some 70 of them marched on Wiveliscombe demanding bread and beer. Later the same year cholera struck the impoverished men and work came to a complete standstill and wasn't restarted until 1870. Built in broad gauge, the line was changed to standard gauge just eight years after it opened; it had cost £21,000 a mile. Worked by the Bristol & Exeter, which became part of the Great Western Railway in 1876, the Devon & Somerset plodded on until 1901 when, along with its £½ million debts, it was purchased by the GWR.

The line had been proposed by local interests and was a truly rural affair. It had eleven stations plus its own terminus in Barnstaple, which had one long platform, a small bay and a modest goods yard.

Though starting in Somerset it entered Devon only to return to Somerset for a while, until some two miles west of Dulverton it re-entered Devon, within whose borders it stayed.

The connection to the Bristol & Exeter was made at Norton Fitzwarren where the Minehead line also joined. This station was rebuilt in 1930 and the track again altered in 1937.

121

Swimbridge was the first stop from Barnstaple and like most stations had double track and a goods shed. (Lens of Sutton Association)

Bishops Nympton seen here in 1966 just two months before the line closed. (Kidderminster Railway Museum)

As one would expect from the geology of Exmoor, the line had plenty of fairly steep gradients, many at 1 in 60, plus three modest tunnels and two viaducts. One of the difficult climbs followed Wiveliscombe station where a 2-mile-long section of 1 in 58 ended with the 445 yd Bathealton tunnel whose restricted bore made it very unpleasant for the engine crew. Next came the Waterrow Viaduct, a lattice girder structure some 162 yds long whose sorry condition probably helped the end to come sooner rather than later.

In 1884 the delightful Exe Valley route joined the line a few miles from Dulverton at Morebath Junction (originally without a station) though the Exe valley trains terminated at Dulverton. A further 4 miles at 1 in 58 brought the trains to the summit of the line at East Anstey 700 ft above sea level. The line was now mainly downhill to Barnstaple. For a brief period between 1874 and 1894 a horse-drawn tramway brought iron ore from the Florence and Croborn mines down the Mole valley to the line near South Molton. The station at South Molton itself was an

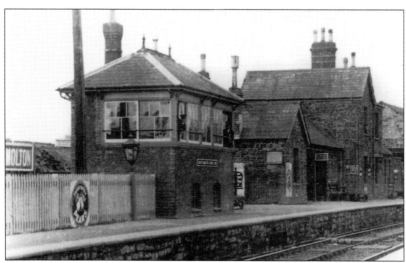

South Molton was one of the busier stations even though the town was over a mile to the south. Today all the trackbed from Barnstaple to here is buried beneath the A361. (Kidderminster Railway Museum)

East Anstey station, probably in the 1960s. At 700 ft this was the highest point on the line. (Lens of Sutton Association)

Dulverton station, potentially the most important station but somewhat spoiled by being two miles from the village. The left-hand platform was used by the Exe Valley trains which terminated here. Today the station and goods shed have been converted into houses but everything else has been flattened. (Kidderminster Railway Museum)

Venn Cross which straddled the Devon/Somerset border, was also a summit point as can be seen in the single track tunnel ahead. (R. G. Nelson)

important and busy one despite being three quarters of a mile from the town. There was once a lively trade in rabbits from South Molton, destined for London. Filleigh Viaduct, some 232 yds long, led to Filleigh station. Formerly called Castle Hill it was changed in 1881 to Filleigh in order to avoid confusion with a similarly named station in west London, known to us today as West Ealing. Like much of the GWR, the line was converted to standard gauge in the 1880s.

The journey time was a leisurely 1¾ hours for the 44½ miles but though most trains stopped at all stations, the line itself was plagued with speed restrictions. Passenger trains could not exceed 30 mph down any of the steep sections nor could they traverse a facing point at more than 10 mph.

Though featured in earlier proposals there was still no link to the LSWR lines in Barnstaple without which the Devon & Somerset could not join in the potentially lucrative traffic to and from Ilfracombe. Following a threat to build its own extension to Ilfracombe, the LSWR agreed to a link, which was put in 1887.

Wiveliscombe station, strictly speaking in Somerset, served its village well. Today the station building still exists as part of private commercial premises. (Kidderminster Railway Museum)

This enabled traffic from Taunton to run into Ilfracombe, a service that carried on until the Ilfracombe line closed.

By the early 1900s the motive power was 2-4-0 tank engines, plus 0-6-0 tender locomotives. Later 0-6-0 pannier tanks joined the motley collection along with steam railcars. Slowly, as the 1930s, passed the 4300 class 2-6-0 tender engines became the norm, the weakness of the viaducts preventing any heavier locomotives being used. The Barnstaple terminus had been renamed Barnstaple Victoria Road in 1949 and its engine shed closed in 1951, after which the GWR engines ran round to the SR facilities where they were turned before returning to home ground. In 1960 heavy rain had flooded the Exeter to Barnstaple line and Southern Region trains for Ilfracombe travelled over the route. The same year saw the closure of the Victoria Road station for passengers with Taunton trains working to and from Barnstaple Junction. In the bad winter of 1962/3 the line provided a vital link to the rural areas, people coming to the stations with sledges to collect supplies brought in by train. Helicopters flew from Dulverton station with provisions for the more remote farms and hamlets on Exmoor.

By 1964 two-car or three-car DMUs were providing most of the local services, the goods traffic having now ceased. The following year saw the last steam-hauled train and just a year later in 1966 the line was closed.

Like so many rural lines the relatively simple construction meant that the trackbed was quickly ploughed under. Only deep cuttings and viaducts lingered on. Most of the line from Barnstaple to South Molton disappeared completely under the new A361 trunk road.

Tiverton to Tiverton Junction

The first branch line opened in the area was the Bristol & Exeter Railway's connection from Tiverton Junction (originally Tiverton Road), on the main Taunton to Exeter line, to Tiverton,

Tiverton station in 1959 with an Exe Valley train ready to depart for Exeter behind a 4500 class 2-6-2 tank engine – powerful stuff for this line! (Kidderminster Railway Museum)

Tiverton Junction on the main Exeter line in 1959. The Tiverton line is curving away to the right. All signs of it have disappeared. (Kidderminster Railway Museum)

some five miles away and opened with broad gauge track in 1848. There was just one intermediate station at Halberton where the line passed beneath the Grand Western Canal, which ironically is still in water though the railway line has long vanished. Originally space was purchased for double track and in the 1960s an enterprising farmer leased the spare track area and planted two rows of apple trees nearly a mile long! Despite Tiverton then being the third largest town in Devon there was very little through traffic from the main line, the service being given a bay platform of its own in 1931. The service became known by the charming nickname of the 'Tivvy Bumper'. Always run by the Bristol & Exeter and later the GWR, the trains were usually one or two coaches worked as an auto train by a 4-4-0 tank engine after the 1931 alterations. Some twelve trains ran on weekdays with up to four on Sundays. The line was converted to standard gauge in 1884 to coincide with the arrival of the Exe Valley lines in Tiverton.

Tiverton Junction station had a separate covered platform for the Tiverton train with its own engine shed and turntable, plus a separate bay for the Hemyock branch. It was completely rebuilt in 1932, giving the branch lines conventional platforms with somewhat mean canopies. The old Tiverton bay became the 'butter' platform – a commodity that had to be handled and dispatched promptly before the days of refrigerated vans.

The passenger service ended in 1964 with goods lingering on until 1967. One of the 1400 class engines used on the line is now housed in the Tiverton Museum, along with interesting photos of the station.

The Exe Valley lines

Though always operated as a single standard gauge line, the route was originally built as two independent lines. The Exe Valley Railway Company opened from Stoke Canon station just 3½ miles from Exeter and followed the river Exe north to Tiverton. Opened in 1885 it was leased to the GWR from the start. The Exe Valley North Railway built its line north from Tiverton, again following the river Exe until taking a minor valley to Bampton and on to a junction with the Taunton–

Thorverton, a busy local station whose traffic included grain for the rail-connected mill nearby. (Kidderminster Railway Museum)

Barnstaple line near Morebath. In a pleasant change from the usual delays, the contractor completed this line nine months early, beating the southern line into Tiverton. Though worked as one line by the GWR, the Exe Valley North company retained its technical independence for a further 20 years. The terminus of the older line from Tiverton Junction was converted to a goods yard and a new Tiverton station built to serve all three lines. This was a busy station and by 1958 had a staff of thirty-eight.

The service started in a bay platform at Exeter St David's station and left the main line and entered its own platform at Stoke Canon. This station was rebuilt twice (1894 and 1932) with passing lines to allow slow traffic to be passed by fast expresses. The first stop away from the main line was Bramford Speke halt soon followed by the much larger Thorverton, with its passing loop, goods shed and further sidings, including one to a mill, which carried grain traffic. Next came two further halts, Up Exe halt and Burn halt, followed by Cadeleigh. This was really the station for Bickleigh but the name was already in use (near Plymouth) and was changed to avoid confusion. The station had a passing loop and a small goods yard. Tiverton West Exe came next, a busy halt, before crossing the Exe for the umpteenth time to reach Tiverton station. As the main station on the line it had two platforms, one of which had a bay for the 'Tivvy Bumper'. There was a large goods yard with sidings for the gasworks, petroleum tanks and coal depots.

The line north had three further stations at Bolham, Cove and Bampton, this last station serving a large village with stone quarrying as its local industry. The quarry was served by a long siding, which passed out of the goods yard, crossed the river and served an interchange siding where the extensive narrow gauge quarry lines ended. The last section then joined the Taunton–Barnstaple line with the service ending at Dulverton.

Much of the line shared the beautiful Exe valley, with the road and the river all fighting for space – so tight was it in places that the road authorities grabbed parts of the rail trackbed as soon as the line closed in order to widen the roadway.

There was a maximum speed of 35 mph on the entire branch. The usual train was a two-coach auto train. This was pulled

Cadeleigh station resplendent with two platforms and goods shed shows how important the railway was to the rural community, there being no villages of any real size for miles. (Kidderminster Railway Museum)

The same station today, renamed Bickleigh and home to the Devon Railway Centre. This tourist attraction includes model railways and a narrow gauge line. (Author)

north by a 1400 class 4-4-0 tank engine, which then pushed its train back to Exeter. Occasionally a pannier tank or a 2-6-2 standard tank would be used. The through journey took a leisurely hour and ten minutes for the 24 miles, having climbed some 500 ft.

The weekday train service was a good nine passenger trains each way plus usually a single mixed goods train. In the summer season a Sunday service ran from Exeter to Tiverton. The inevitable decline in traffic occurred during the 1950s and 60s and with no real through traffic to sustain it, the lines were closed in a piecemeal manner. First to go in 1963 was the main section from Thorverton to Morebath Junction, followed in 1966 by the Exeter to Thorverton section. The last to go was the first built – the route of the 'Tivvy Bumper', which closed in 1967.

Most stations are now private residences but Tiverton has completely disappeared below new road works. Bampton's goods yard is now a small factory estate but alas, the station has been buried beneath a car park. Bickleigh (formerly Cadeleigh) is now the Devon Railway Centre with the station still standing and a variety of railway related exhibits.

The Hemyock branch – the Culm Valley line

Originally authorised in 1873 as a light railway, the promoters of the Hemyock branch, mostly local farmers and landowners, had hoped for a total construction bill of around £30,000. Everything was planned for simplicity; only one cottage needed to be purchased and removed over the entire route. The *Railway News* stated that the works were so simple that six months would suffice to construct the line. Only one objector was known and though there was debate about the best position for Hemyock station, the project looked straightforward. The Bristol & Exeter Railway was helpful and indeed undertook to run the line for the usual 50% of gross receipts. All this enthusiasm was to end in tears as problem after problem arose.

Uffculme station in 1947, with 4800 class tank engine No 4827 ready to continue to Tiverton Junction. (Lens of Sutton Association)

It is interesting to note that the population of the area at this time was barely 6,500 but it had been the farming interest that was the main drive. The original contractor, a Mr Jardine, was sacked after barely six months' work and the railway company asked a Mr Broome to undertake the completion as assistant manager. By mid 1875 he had relinquished the task and Mr Pain, the company's engineer, took over control. The work so far completed was of a very poor quality and much had to be redone; the contractors had been plagued by unreliable locomotives and the weather had not been very kind. Built in standard gauge it finally opened in 1876, having cost nearly £50,000 and to make matters worse the early traffic was about half of that expected. The owners decided to cut their losses and sold the line to the GWR in 1880 for a mere £33,000.

Passenger traffic was always light and just four trains (often mixed) each day sufficed, with no Sunday service. There was an overall speed limit of 15 mph, which caused problems as the generators on some of the old coaches couldn't charge the coach

Culmstock, with a very similar layout to Uffculme, both stations serving their villages well. Both, alas, completely gone today. (Kidderminster Railway Museum)

batteries at these low speeds, an overnight battery charger being used instead. The numerous tight curves also meant that push-pull auto coach working could not be permitted, all locomotives having to run around their vehicles before returning.

There were four intermediate stations. The first at Coldharbour halt was kept busy with coal for the adjacent woollen mill for many years. Uffculme station was well placed for the village and had goods facilities and a siding that serviced the local grain mill built in 1935. The third station was for Culmstock and was very similar to Uffculme. The fourth was a small halt at Whitehall, with a short siding serving a local grain mill. Hemyock station boasted an engine shed and a carriage shed, plus a cattle pen and a long siding, which crossed over a road to feed a corn mill. It was this mill that was later taken over in 1886 by the Culm Valley Dairy Co though it continued to produce animal feed as well as butter and cheese. In 1920 it was joined by the Cow & Gate condensed milk factory served

134

by another siding, which crossed the same road 50 yds or so further south.

The older crossing was odd in that the gates shut across the track but not the road, so locomotives were not allowed to cross. Trucks had to be pushed until the engine just reached the road, after which the trucks were winched into the old mill site. The later crossing to the Cow & Gate factory had gates that protected the road and locos could complete the movement. On both sidings gravity was used to bring the wagons back into the station area. The milk processing included using centrifugal separators to separate the cream, becoming in 1888 the first mechanised butter factory in the West, though by 1916 it reverted to just milk production. In 1927 United Dairies became the first company to use glass lined, 3,000 gallon, tank wagons to convey milk. The change was quite dramatic with each tank wagon replacing three wagons, which previously would have carried 176 separate milk churns.

Hemyock in 1960, well after the engine and carriage sheds had vanished. Both the mill and dairy are now buried beneath a new housing estate. (Lens of Sutton Association)

Prior to 1932, when Tiverton Junction was completely rebuilt, a somewhat precarious system was used to get the engine around the train as there was no run round loop provided. The engine would push its empty coaches back up the branch line, which rose as it left the station. The guard would apply his brake then the loco would uncouple from the coaches and move into a short spur. The points reset, the guard would let the coaches run back into the platform under gravity and once they had stopped the loco would emerge from the little spur and couple up to the end coach, now being at the front of the departing train. After 1932 a conventional run round loop was provided. A mixture of odd locomotives had been used on the line until 1932 when Collett's little 0-4-2 tank engines appeared and these served the line to the end of steam.

Passenger numbers declined and, by the 1950s, each train managed only around five passengers. Goods traffic, which had peaked in the 1930s at around 26,000 tons, had dropped to less than half this by 1960, with livestock movement being all but ended. All the usual economies were applied but there was no way the passenger service could ever pay and so, in 1963, the service ended but the milk traffic was still good. All the stations were demolished by 1971. In 1968 British Rail strengthened the track to take class 2 and 3 diesels, but although the traffic had reached over 30,000 gallons a day, the transporting of milk ceased in 1975 when Unigate announced it was closing its factory. Fuel oil was conveyed for a further month but the line closed completely the same year and all the track was lifted by 1977. The connection to the main line has now disappeared under the M5 as it thunders its way past the old Tiverton Junction site, which now operates just as passing loops. The 'park and ride' station Tiverton Parkway, for commuters to Exeter and Taunton, was built more than a mile further north. At the Hemyock end, a car park has been built over the old station site.

9
To the Seaside by the Southern Railway

The Sidmouth branch
Tipton St Johns to Exmouth
The Seaton branch
Axminster to Lyme Regis

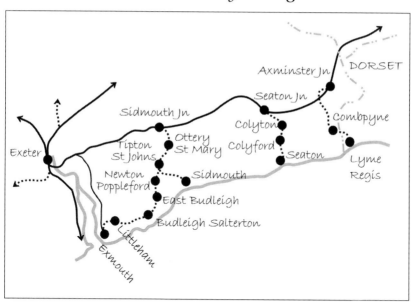

The Sidmouth branch

Sidmouth has always been select, encouraging the retiring well-off since the very earliest times; in 1805 it even had a theatre. Though it was happy to have the services of a railway branch, it didn't want it to bring in the hordes of holidaymakers that would shatter its carefully nurtured peace and quiet, so the station was positioned a full mile from the town centre and the beach. Like Seaton and Beer, Sidmouth had toyed with the idea of a harbour and work was even started but it came to naught. We must remember that during the 1800s there was a long-established service of small ships that plied along the coast carrying both goods and passengers to and from Exeter and Plymouth so these harbour-building ideas were not just idle speculation.

The first attempt at a railway line was by the Sidmouth Railway and Harbour Co who obtained their Act in 1862 but collapsed, with nothing built, in 1869. A fresh start was made two years later when the Sidmouth Railway Co. started to build the line. The LSWR was to work the line from the start but didn't absorb the branch line company until 1922 prior to the creation of the Southern Railway. The branch trains began running in 1874 from Sidmouth Junction (originally Feniton, then called Ottery Road in 1861, then Ottery St Mary in 1868 and, finally,

Ottery St Mary station in the early 1960s. The signal box was unusual in having the lever frame facing the back wall instead of the windows. (Kidderminster Railway Museum)

138

Tipton St Johns with a DMU from Sidmouth approaching in 1964. The signal box was a replacement opened in 1897 in readiness for the new branch to Budleigh. The hideous water tank was built on the site of the old signal box. (Kidderminster Railway Museum)

Sidmouth Junction when the branch opened) on the LSWR main line to Exeter, which had opened in 1860. After the branch closed Sidmouth Junction reverted to the name Feniton, having come full circle. This early name changing also included Tipton as it was originally called. Confusion with Tipton in the West Midlands caused St Johns to be added in 1881.

Sidmouth Junction provided a bay for the branch trains, plus a goods shed and a turntable though this was removed in the 1930s. After leaving the main line the branch stayed almost level for just over a half mile and then dropped for nearly a mile at 1 in 53 to reach the valley of the river Otter. A gentle descent took it through Ottery St Mary and into Tipton St Johns where it was faced with the climb between the Beacon and Bulverton hills. This took 1½ miles at 1 in 45 followed by an almost equally steep descent into the outskirts of Sidmouth. These gradients meant a strict limit on the early locomotives and the need for goods

139

Sidmouth station in 1964 with a lonely DMU awaiting passengers. The engine shed had been used by an engineering company for many years when this shot was taken. Though 200 ft above and 1 mile from the town the station goods yard was extensive and usually busy. (Kidderminster Railway Museum)

trains to have a 20-ton brake van, preferably fitted with sanding gear. Ottery St Mary station had two platforms and was extended in 1936 to cope with the long holiday trains. It had a new signal box in 1955, built on the opposite platform but still next to the level crossing. Nearby were the gasworks, a sawmill and a paper factory. Tipton St Johns, though a smaller village, had a similar station including a 33-lever signal box and a level crossing. This was the junction for the Exmouth branch and originally trains could be directed into either platform though this facility seems to have been removed by 1926. The railway inspector on the opening of the Exmouth branch insisted on a footbridge between the two platforms as it was now a junction station.

Sidmouth station boasted an island platform and a goods shed, plus a turntable and engine shed, though engines were no longer serviced here after the 1930s and the shed was converted

140

for use by an engineering company. As so often happened, the original wooden engine shed burnt down and was replaced by a brick structure. There were three substantial sidings and a 23-lever signal box, which survived unaltered to the end. The local gasworks was also nearby and its coal was brought in by rail until the 1950s.

The passenger service was always buoyant, opening with seven weekday trains, which soon increased to sixteen on weekdays and thirteen on Sundays. Even in 1965 the DMU service made fourteen trips with ten on Sundays, though this fell to seven and six respectively in the last year of service, 1966/7. The Sidmouth Junction to Tipton section had additional traffic that went on to Exmouth, making this section one of the busiest single lines in Devon. There was also considerable through traffic, including coaches from London. In addition, on weekdays there was a daily goods train. Locomotives included T1 (0-4-4), M7 (0-4-4), class 2 (2-6-2) and occasionally the Bullied West Country Pacifics.

The difficulty of making these seaside branch lines pay can be understood if we consider the passenger numbers in 1964. Typical winter weekday passengers – 40, which rose to around

Sidmouth station today, virtually complete and in use as a garage and residence. The goods yard has been used for an industrial estate. (Author)

100 in the summer (remember, that's still barely four people per train) but summer Saturdays could produce up to 900 passengers. With these figures it's hardly surprising that the end came in 1967.

Tipton St Johns to Exmouth

Exmouth was a thriving town by 1846 when the Bristol & Exeter Railway's line towards Dawlish edged its way along the western side of the river Exe. Trains would have been clearly visible in Exmouth and a demand for a rail link was inevitable. An 1855 scheme had been proposed by Brunel which was to leave the Bristol & Exeter line at Exminster, cross the Exe on a massive bridge to Topsham and then continue down the eastern side of the river and into Exmouth. However, like so many early schemes, it came to naught. In 1860 the LSWR had reached Exeter and within a year a branch from its line had been opened to Exmouth, whose population was now around 6,000. Worked

Newton Poppleford station, built some two years after the line went into service, had a single platform and one long siding on which two camping coaches resided in the 40s and 50s. Seen here in 1950 still handling coal for the local area. (Stations UK)

East Budleigh in 1950. The station served Otterton across the river valley better than its namesake. (Stations UK)

by the LSWR from the start, it included a short branch to the Exmouth docks. Further east the Sidmouth branch had been opened, also from the LSWR main line in 1874, but had left the river Otter valley at Tipton St Johns. Further down this valley were three villages, Newton Poppleford, Otterton and Budleigh Salterton, the last being of a considerable size. A locally sponsored branch known as the Budleigh Salterton Railway was authorised in 1894 to serve these villages and opened in 1897. In 1903 the LSWR extended this line to Exmouth to join the existing Exeter–Exmouth line it had built in 1861. Though barely five miles in length the route of this last section was much more difficult than the straight flat run from Tipton St Johns, including a long viaduct forced on them by local Exmouth residents who didn't want a railway line near their area. There was now a separate route for summer trains to Exmouth, which avoided Exeter, and indeed many through trains from London to Exmouth took this option.

143

Budleigh Salterton, seen here around 1930, was the most important stop on the line and indeed had been the terminus for six years from the opening of the branch in 1897. The village spread to the left of the picture. (Stations UK)

Littleham in 1958 was roughly halfway down the 1 in 50 descent into Exmouth and its track included catch points to arrest any wayward trains. There was a considerable goods yard on the right behind the platform. (Stations UK)

144

Exmouth station originally had two platform faces, an engine shed and turntable plus the little line to the docks. This ran along the edge of the estuary for about ½ mile and fed three sidings around the basin. Exmouth station was rebuilt in 1924 with four platform faces, a better goods yard and, using land reclaimed from the sea, a realigned route for the dock branch. In 1927 the engine shed was rebuilt and served right through to the end of steam in 1963. The large 70-lever signal box had the unusual feature of a balcony that extended on both sides to enable the signalman to exchange tokens with the locomotive crews as they passed in and out of the station. This meant that the trains didn't have to come almost to a halt, though the later DMUs needed the signalman to come down to ground level to perform the same task. Exmouth station was reduced to a modern single platform building in 1976, with the goods yard and harbour line all built over.

The service started with eight weekday trains, which soon grew to around the ten to twelve mark for the rest of the life of the branch. Sunday services started in the 1920s and stayed at around four to six trains. During its life several variations were tried, with trains running from Sidmouth to Exeter via Exmouth; some started at Sidmouth Junction and some at Budleigh. The journey from Tipton St Johns to Exmouth took typically 30 minutes.

Trains, usually of two coaches, were hauled by the trusty LSWR O2 and M7 tank locomotives. By the 1950s class 2, 3 and 4 tank engines were in use plus, in the 1960s, the inevitable DMUs.

Unlike so many branch lines, the route took the trouble to get close to its villages, crossing over the river to reach Newton Poppleford just 1½ miles from Tipton. The far smaller hamlet of Colaton Raleigh was provided with a siding in the 1930s. Otterton and East Budleigh shared a station, which although called East Budleigh was in fact on the edge of Otterton, a full mile from its namesake. It was provided with a goods siding and cattle pens and later two camping coaches. Budleigh Salterton station was within the town but positioned to the north, some ½ mile from the centre. Built as a terminus it boasted a small goods yard, cattle pens and a modest engine shed. A second platform was added, possibly in anticipation of the LSWR's extension, which enabled trains to pass. Apart from a short section at 1 in 50 to reach Budleigh station, the route so far was a gentle descent. The extension to Exmouth was mostly at 1 in 50, climbing to a summit near Knowle and then descending into the existing station at Exmouth via just one station at Littleham. This had two platforms and a small goods yard, plus long sidings used to hold holiday coaching stock only needed for the long distance Saturday trains.

In 1936 no fewer than 18,500 people travelled from Waterloo to Exmouth, most of whom would have been summer holidaymakers.

The post-war Saturday holiday trains are quite extraordinary to our eyes today. They were often fourteen or more coaches long and covered very long journeys. As an example, the Southern Railway seaside resorts were served by a through train that started at Cleethorpes, travelled via Grimsby, Lincoln, Nottingham and after five hours of travel reached Birmingham. From here it progressed via Gloucester, Bath and the Somerset and Dorset line, eventually reaching Budleigh Salterton and Exmouth some 10½ hours after it set off.

A view of Exmouth station looking down the platforms towards Exeter and Budleigh taken around 1930. This shows the station at its maximum size with a vast array of signals. (Stations UK)

As part of measures to cut costs in 1961 the ticket office at Littleham was built as an extension to the signal box, enabling just one member of staff to run the station. Many of the stations had camping coaches, but in 1961 Tipton St Johns could boast a former Pullman coach, proudly called a 'holiday coach'.

Though opened late, the branch fed useful traffic into Exmouth, which had grown faster than any other Devon town reaching some 14,000 in the 1930s and nearly 30,000 by 1990. Like the Sidmouth line, it closed to freight in 1964 and to passengers in 1967. Though, as if to protest, nature flooded the line near Newton Poppleford in 1968, holding up the dismantling work.

The Seaton branch

The Seaton & Beer Railway Company obtained its Act in 1863 and five years later the service started, though all mention of Beer was quietly dropped. Originally, Axmouth, a mile or so up

Seaton Junction photographed from the window of a departing train as the Seaton train simmers at its platform. (R. K. Blencowe)

the river estuary, had been a busy port but its trade virtually ceased once the line was opened and 10 years later the river mouth was bridged, cutting off the port for good. Both Seaton and Beer had fostered hopes of building a harbour but nothing came of it once the railway arrived.

The line was fairly straightforward in engineering terms with under a mile of 1 in 76, a mile at 1 in 100 and the rest almost level. The junction with the main line, at Seaton Junction, started off with the branch trains having to leave the bay platform and then reverse to enter the branch, the same performance being needed for trains coming from Seaton. A mere 59 years later, in 1927, a separate platform was erected just for the Seaton branch as part of a major rebuild.

The passenger service was good; initially just five trains ran on weekdays but this soon increased until in the 1930s there was a service of twelve trains every day. Seaton station was rebuilt by the Southern Railway in 1937 and it enjoyed considerable

Colyton station in its new guise as the northern end of the tramway. The station building is substantially original except for the ornate canopy and the health and safety railings. (Author)

Colyford was always a small, single platform station. Here a BR class 2 with two ex-GWR auto coaches arrives from the Junction in 1963. (J. H. Aston)

Seaton terminus in 1950. The main platform with a run round line is on the left with the shorter bay on the right. Note the classic Southern Railway concrete lamp posts. (Stations UK)

Saturday holiday traffic for some years. By the 1950s the service was thirteen weekday trains and six on Sunday and, except for the occasional variation, this level of service continued right through until 1965. Despite this good service, passengers were no longer using the line, which, when all is said and done, didn't take you anywhere useful! Seaton Junction was merely a point at which to change to the main line services for Exeter or Axminster. In 1963 the through coaches from London stopped and the following year freight services were withdrawn; by 1966 it was all over and the line closed.

The station was close to the beach, the gasworks and a holiday camp and the town centre was a flat half mile walk, a feature that, apart from Exmouth, was unique in Devon. It would have been easy to have sited the station nearer the centre but, in a strange act of optimism, the railway had kept the station near the estuary and constructed a toll bridge across the river in the hope of attracting traffic from the totally rural area to the east.

A variety of locomotives were used over the years but the mainstay was the hard working M7 0-4-4 tank engines. The charming old 0415 class locos took charge of one train on Saturdays for a while, whilst in earlier years Brighton-built D1 tanks, displaced by electrification of the lines south of London in the 1930s, were regularly used. Seaton had a small engine shed (rebuilt and moved some time after 1905) but no turntable. Ex-LSWR O2s also saw service, as did U class locomotives on occasional excursion runs. DMUs arrived in 1963 along with a change to the Western Region of British Rail who also used pannier tanks and the larger class 2s. Mixed trains of goods and passenger coaches were used from the earliest times and auto trains ran from the 1930s until the end of steam.

The two intermediate stations served Colyton and Colyford but the line was laid on the eastern side of the valley whereas both villages were on the western side, adding that distance factor that puts people off.

The trackbed, however, rose from the ashes in 1970 when it was acquired by Mr Claude Lane who transferred his Eastbourne Tramway to the new larger site. The older Eastbourne-built trams were re-gauged from 2 ft to 2 ft 9 in and new trams have been added, built in the workshops that are on the old Seaton standard gauge railway site. Trams now happily rumble along the estuary to Colyton throughout the normal summer season. The Seaton end of the tramway leaves the old railway bed as it nears Seaton and skirts around the former holiday camp site to a terminus nearer the town.

Axminster to Lyme Regis

Lyme Regis had started life as a port and during the early 1800s slowly evolved into a seaside resort. Several schemes to link it to the main rail system failed, including the Lyme Regis Railway Company, which actually started work in 1874 before disappearing into the dust. Eventually a local company obtained an order to build the Axminster & Lyme Regis Light Railway in 1899 and the route opened in 1903. Though Lyme Regis is in Dorset, the majority of the line is in Devon and so is included here. The line was operated by the LSWR from the start and due to the poor financial position of the original company, the LSWR took over the line completely in 1907. Conventional signalling and heavier track was installed, after which the line settled down to a life as a typical branch line. The geology of the area is both varied and interesting but in turn posed problems connected with the cuttings and the only viaduct. Concrete had been shipped in via the harbour for the construction of the ten-arch Cannington Viaduct near Combpyne. As construction progressed, it was found that the first two pillars, nearest Axminster, had settled, putting a strain on the arch between pillars 2 and 3 so this arch had to be quickly reinforced by a jack arch, which gave the whole structure a strange hump at one end.

Once the line had opened, the harbour rapidly declined. The only intermediate station was at Combpyne, where visitors in 1908 came to see the massive landslip between Lyme Regis and Seaton when the ground caught fire and burned for eight months, a somewhat unusual but welcome boost to traffic.

The passenger service was fairly steady, starting with six trains, rising to eight in 1907 and reaching eleven by 1938, after

151

Axminster Junction with a loco taking water before running around its train. (R. K. Blencowe)

The scene today. The footbridge and water tank have gone and the island platform is now deserted and overgrown. (Author)

Combpyne station in 1956 having lost the right-hand platform and its signal box. (Brunel University/Mowat Collection)

which the service stayed at around nine or ten trains per day until closure. Sunday services were much poorer, not even starting until 1930, and in winter reverting to buses from 1950. Through coaches from London ran during the 1953–1963 period. Though some trains were mixed, a goods only train ran each day.

The 6¾ mile long line included over 3 miles at a gradient of 1 in 40, plus several sections of sharp curves, which made it a considerable challenge for the locomotives. Early locomotives were the A1 Brighton 'Terrier' class and the LSWR O2s beloved of the Isle of Wight in post-war years. Both suffered twisted frames and severe tyre wear. In 1913 the LSWR Adams 0415 class radial 4-4-2 tanks were tried, although already 25 years old, and they became the most successful engine for the line, lasting until 1961. In the 1930s ex-Brighton D1s ran for a while; later class 1400 GWR 0-4-2 tanks were tried but again couldn't cope with the tight bends. Following some relaying of track, BR class 2 tanks appeared from 1960 before DMUs took over for the final years. Until the class 2 locomotives arrived, it was standard practice to double head the longer holiday season trains.

Axminster Junction had two rather unusual features. The branch line left from a bay platform on the 'up' or northern side of the station and immediately climbed in order to cross over the main lines, before setting off southwards towards the coast. The goods yard occupied the other side and presumably was considered too established to be altered for the branch, though there was a connection from the branch into the yard until 1915. The second feature was the massive water tank built at the end of the bay line, which included a steam engine to pump water up from the river Axe. This fed water to all the water columns on the station. Combpyne was reached after 4¼ gruelling miles of climbing. Originally provided with an island platform and a passing line, it was reduced to just a single platform face in 1930, the truncated loop being used as a long siding for the occasional goods wagon. Combpyne also had a solitary unheated camping coach parked at the end of this siding.

The station at Lyme Regis had just the one full platform, plus a short bay, which was later lengthened. In addition there were three sidings, a goods shed and a wooden engine shed. The latter burnt down in 1912 and was replaced by an asbestos-clad

Though much of the trackbed has disappeared Cannington Viaduct still stands today. The jack arch at the far end can be clearly seen. (Author)

Lyme Regis station, probably in the 1950s, with a single coach in the bay used for the summer Saturday through service to Waterloo. (R. K. Blencowe)

building that lasted until 1963 and the end of steam. The goods shed was repositioned from the end of the sidings to a position that allowed a train of goods wagons to be handled rather than just a single van.

There is a delightful story told of an elderly lady who departed from Lyme Regis sitting in what she believed to be a through coach but alas, it wasn't, and she was duly taken back to Lyme Regis. The staff telephoned Axminster to explain the problem, asking that someone meet her and ensure she caught the appropriate main line train. Unfortunately the message never reached the platform staff and the poor lady endured another journey to Axminster and back to Lyme Regis – her comments are not recorded!

The station at Lyme Regis was some 250 ft above sea level and ¾ mile from the town centre, resulting in good business for the taxis but, alas, a walk that would discourage regular travellers. Like so many of the lines in this book, this one enabled the expansion and modernisation of the communities it served but once the motor car and lorry were established there was no way it could compete. The line was closed in 1965.

Conclusion

Looking at today's railway map of Devon, one wonders if anyone lives there! There is just one main line linking Exeter, Torbay and Plymouth to the rest of the country and feeding the only rail link into Cornwall. Plus, there is one single, subsidised line from Waterloo to Barnstaple via Exeter and a tiny, heavily subsidised line sneaking north from Plymouth to Bere Alston and just across the county border to Gunnislake. I almost forgot – there's the busy commuter line to Exmouth still showing what might have been with a little more imagination.

What is hard to realise is that this apparently empty county is exactly what Devon would have been if there hadn't been a mass of other, long gone railway lines, for virtually every large village or town grew and survived due to the railways – they were the commercial lifelines of the county for over 100 years. The early main lines had been built by 'up country' bankers and merchants who could see the profit to be made by linking major towns and cities with the new-fangled railway. Almost everything else was sponsored by local people wanting to join in the prosperity – and what a good job they did!

The decline of these rural lines had started as soon as cars and lorries appeared but the demise of these lines was to some extent held at bay by the two world wars when the national need to move vast numbers of troops and great quantities of materials kept the lines busy. Afterwards, seemingly without any thanks or recognition, the rural network was closed down. But, thanks to preserved steam railways (Devon has two excellent examples), we can still experience the noise, smells and excitement of our early local lines.

Today some of the lines have become cycle paths and walking routes and a few of the old stations are still with us in a wide variety of guises. The rest now only form strange, lonely embankments or vague dips in the fields but hopefully this book will have painted in at least some of the original, hard working lines that served Devon's vast and beautiful rural areas.

Opening and Final Closure Dates of Lines to Regular Passenger Traffic

Line	Opened	Final Closure	
Tiverton Jn/Tiverton	12. 6.1848	5.10.1964	
Barnstaple/Fremington	1. 8.1854	2.10.1965	
Plymouth/Tavistock	21. 6.1859	31.12.1962	†
Fremington/Bideford	2. 3.1855	2.10.1965	
Paignton/Kingswear	18. 8.1864	28.10.1972	†
Tavistock/Launceston	1. 6.1865	31.12.1962	
Newton Abbot/Moreton	4. 7.1866	28. 2.1959	
Churston/Brixham	28. 2.1868	13. 5.1963	
Seaton Jn/Seaton	16. 3.1868	7. 3.1966	
Exeter/Okehampton	3.10.1871	5. 6.1972	
Totnes/Ashburton	1. 5.1872	3.11.1958	†
Bideford/Torrington	18. 7.1872	2.10.1965	
Taunton/Barnstaple	1.11.1873	3.10.1966	
Sidmouth Jn/Sidmouth	6. 7.1874	6. 3.1967	
Barnstaple/Ilfracombe	30. 7.1874	5.10.1970	
Okehampton/Lydford	12.10.1874	6. 5.1968	†
Tiverton Jn/Hemyock	29. 5.1876	9. 9.1963	
Okehampton/Holsworthy	20. 1.1879	3.10.1966	
Heathfield/Christow	9.10.1882	7. 6.1958	
Yelverton/Princetown	11. 8.1883	5. 3.1956	
Exeter/Dulverton	1. 5.1885	7.10.1963	
Halwill/Launceston	21. 7.1886	3.10.1966	
Lydford/Plymouth(LSWR)	2. 6.1890	6. 5.1968	*
Plymouth/Turnchapel	5. 9.1897	10. 9.1951	
Brent/Kingsbridge	19.12.1893	16. 9.1963	
Tipton/Budleigh Salterton	15. 5.1897	6. 3.1967	
Plymouth/Yealmpton	17. 1.1898	7.10.1947	
Lynton/Barnstable	11. 5.1898	29. 9.1935	
Holsworthy/Bude	10. 8.1898	3.10.1966	
Budleigh Salterton/Exmouth	1. 6.1903	6. 3.1967	
Christow/Exeter	1. 7.1903	7. 6.1958	
Axminster/Lyme Regis	24. 8.1903	29.11.1965	
Bere Alston/Callington	2. 3.1908	5.11.1966	*
Bideford/West' Ho!/Appledore	1. 5.1908	28. 3.1917	
Halwill/Torrington	27. 7.1925	1. 3.1965	

† Part of the line is now a preserved steam railway.
* The Plymouth/Bere Alston/Gunnislake section is still open.

Bibliography

Many publications were consulted in the writing of this book and many happy hours were spent poring over Ordnance Survey maps, both old and new. The following selection is believed to still be in print and readily available:

Kingdom, A.R. and Lang, M. *The Newton Abbot to Moretonhampstead Railway* (ARK Publications (Railways))

Kingdom, A.R. *The Plymouth Tavistock and Launceston Railway* (ARK Publications)

Maggs, C. *The Culm Valley Light Railway* (Oakwood Press)

Mitchell, V. and Smith, K. *Branch Line Series* (Middleton Press)

Pomroy, L.W. *The Teign Valley Line* (Oxford Publishing)

Potts, C.R. *The Brixham Branch* (Oakwood Press)

St John Thomas, D. *Regional History of the Railways of Great Britain Vol 1* (David & Charles)

Smith, M. *An Illustrated History of Exmoor's Railways* (Irwell Press)

INDEX